A VICTORY MARCH

My Pathway and Story

of

Grace and Encouragement

By

John J. Klein

*Author of "Your Pathway to Personal Enrichment
& Vocational Enlightenment"*

Copyright © 2016 by John J Klein

A Victory March
By John J Klein

Printed in the United States of America

ISBN 978-0-9971687-0-9

All rights reserved solely by the author. No part of this book may be reproduced in any form without the permission of the author. The views expressed in this book are those of the author.

Foreword by Colin Comerford

Final Publishing Details:
Becky Norwood - Spotlight On Your Business

Dedicated

to

Connie Klein

(Dear, you remain in my heart)

and

Joey Lautzenhiser

(Joey, your young heart touched others before and after your passing)

My promises to both of you are now fulfilled.

TABLE OF CONTENTS

Foreword 1
Acknowledgments 3
Introduction 5
1. Boyhood 7
2. Middle School 14
3. High School 21
4. World of Work: Rookie Year 30
5. World of Work: Growing Pains and Gains 34
6. World of Work Morphs Into Personal Enrichment
   & Vocational Enlightenment 42
7. Families of Another Name 44
8. Author's Interlude 54
9. First Career Crisis and Personal Passages 61
10. World of Work: Banking Leaves Me 81
11. World of Work: Blue Collar Time 88
12. World of Work: Public Sector 93
13. World of Work: Kleinmark, L.L.C. 110
14. Connie and Cancer 116
15. Connie's Victory March 121
16. Victory! Moving On, Marching Forward 134
17. The Encourager's Top Ten Guiding Principles 142
Testimonials 144
Other Publications By John J. Klein 147

FOREWORD

It shouldn't be so difficult.
Every one of us has had this thought at one point or another. Life is never short on ways to startle you, bringing you low only to send you upward, and then careening you into uncharted territory. If anyone knows this, it is John Klein.

I met John as a young man working at a retail store, where I was happy to have a paycheck and be able to interact with interesting people on the job. What I was not prepared for was making a life-long friend. The first time we met outside of work, we went to play mini-golf, and though I can't remember who won (Yes, John won, all right? Could you not rub it in? Let's just move on. No, I'm not still upset. It's fine.), I can remember hearing only a few details of what is now contained in this book, and being astonished. Even in those small moments, however, it was never a woeful story. The saddest and the happiest details alike were talked of gratefully, and honestly. That very night I reaffirmed my commitment to a major life decision because of a few small things he happened to mention about his own commitments. He, of course, didn't know any of this. We were merely getting to know one another. But some stories have more impact than others. This is one of them.

We have stayed great friends through the years. I was incredibly humbled when asked to write this foreword, being merely a friend who has been a relatively brief participant in his tale. But perhaps a friend is best qualified to introduce this march, as I know the incredible man that it took to make it victorious. He wasn't born ready, or given each tool and gadget needed to save himself at every crises; rather he had a smile and faith, and it took him farther than anything else could. I know this because I've seen it and been a part of it, and have been inspired, humored, and most of all encouraged. This book does the same. It is a story of John's life: his trials, losses, and victories. It's his own path, described so that it might illuminate your own.

- Colin Comerford

ACKNOWLEDGMENTS

Writing this book was not easy. It brought back many unpleasant and painful memories. For years I've had people – some rather influential – tell me my story was compelling and that it was a "powerful impact story." While not easy to put one's self out there for public scrutiny, my trust in the Lord is greater than my personal demons. In the autumn of my years, now is the time to pass along what others have taught me. All in all, it's been a lesson in grace.

First and foremost, my gratitude to my Lord Jesus. Many thanks to those who gave their generous and kind testimonials on my behalf, as their trust is forever appreciated. As always, I am reminded that when we hold a torch to light another's path, our own is made that much brighter.

Telling my story could not have been possible without the encouragement and expert proofreading of a special young friend in my life, a much better writer than myself – Colin Comerford.

Thanks also to other proofreaders and editors, Sarah and Kirk Gagliardo and Frank Kitchen, nationally known motivator, author and speaker. A very personal expression of gratitude is extended to my nephew, Seth Thompson. His empathy and background in journalism were encouraging to the encourager. Editing is tedious and sometimes bruising to the ego but needed to maintain objectivity and efficiency. All of you were awesome with your unique perspectives and suggestions.

I'd like to acknowledge, publishing consultant Becky Norwood (Spotlight on Your Business), who has been a godsend. Becky, your brand of encouragement & expertise has been invaluable. You made this project go from good to great! Thank you, Flight Media team of S. Ferullo & J. Coffy, & Toni Steffen for website development.

If this acknowledgment was an acceptance speech for a Grammy the music would be playing. There are so many other people to thank, but let's just say all the people mentioned in my book played a supportive role, directly or indirectly, in the creation of this body of work.

A shout out to my sons, Doug and Steven Klein, Nick Wahl (whose friendship and golfing instructions cannot be overstated), Matt Belt (whose willingness to learn and break bread with me kept me good company and in positive spirits), nephew Tim and Brandy Lowery for loving me and asking me about my progress, honorary nephew Clif McGilvray for his love and faith in my guidance, Joshua Wittig, for his friendship and belief in my personal ministry, Devin Pollick for returning "access" when added energy was needed, Anthony Perez for being faithful and believing in me, Adam Jezeski for making a timely entrance on the stage of my life during an untimely surgery and for making my point about grace and a torch, accompanied with his servant's heart and an entire new perspective on healthy eating and to Tyler Suddarth for his friendship and genuine prayer line to God.

Then lastly, there's Josiah W., Charlie K., Dru H., John S. and others like them, that for whom without my purpose and motivation would have waned – for it is they seeing me as a father-figure - not unlike those who did the same for me when I was young – that reminded me this book is about them, not me. I can only pray the lessons learned and guiding principles serve everyone well. I am blessed.

- John J. Klein

INTRODUCTION

From the beginning books were my first friends. I never felt alone when reading a good book. A man alone I have been off and on during my challenging, yet fortuitous life. Many times I've been told that I have a powerful impact story: One that needs to be told. For years I've resisted telling my story out of reluctance to revisit the scorched earth of my past or fretting that I'll be perceived as one who is playing the victim card. Having said that, there have been times when even I find my story hard to reckon. We all have a story, don't we? Mine is a bit out of the ordinary.

Mine is a love story. I love life! In the simplest of terms, that is my philosophy. And I love the people in my life. I am blessed. I am a man of deep faith and guiding principles. This is a story…a Victory March in which I invite you – the reader – to join me. The following pages highlight some of the passages of my life, one I consider well-lived, in spite of insurmountable odds at times. From childhood to adulthood I would have good people enter and exit my life, as if in a school play where and when a timely key character might enter stage left or right, then part ways or remain for another scene. Unfortunately, misfortune – if not evil (a word I do not use lightly) – commanded my stage, often making me feel powerless and unworthy. Thank God, God was in control.

God prepared me well to become a life and career coach. In 2003 I published *Your Pathway to Personal Enrichment & Vocational Enlightenment*. The book featured (if not branded) the art of encouragement. I am fond of telling people that I am not a therapist or a theologian. I am, indeed, "The Encourager." I earned that title! It was inspired by the name of a newsletter written by a nationally known major league baseball player, whose own comeback story touched my life during the 1980's.

Now, as an older gentleman, without doubt, that moniker will be my legacy. Just as when I am when life coaching, it is my heart's desire that this book be like your temporary best friend, gently nudging your spirit to eventually soar. A writing companion and good friend of mine calls it "bringing beauty to the world." It is my intention that this book will both entertain and inform you as I also share what I call "Lessons Learned from the University of Life" (the title of my modest speaking series). Life is an adventure! My adventure is one of exploring and developing my religious beliefs and personal philosophies, which became "guiding principles" for me to live by.

It is my expectation and mission for readers to find new learning and spiritual awakening from sharing my story…my victory march of grace and encouragement.

BOYHOOD

I *don't belong.*
I don't fit in.

My victory march began with those thoughts as a young boy. The idea of not belonging or fitting in would foreshadow other life passages, all the way into my adulthood. Abraham Maslow, noted American psychologist, would have had a field day with my story. Because of God's grace, I did not want to belong or fit in. Those who would have custody of me had values foreign to my intuitive understanding. That intuition would blossom, and be nurtured for years to come because of good schooling and the positive, loving influence of others outside my home environment and family history. It was grace in action.

Consequently, much of my boyhood was spent as a loner. Most childhood pictures depict me in deep thought, often brooding and extremely sensitive. Later in life, maturity would make "not belonging" a noble goal – when belonging meant compromising ethical standards and moral purpose.

My first awareness of not belonging or fitting in was on the kitchen floor. I was a foster child, barely nine, going on ten years old (when kids, we're always saying one-half a year older or some age going on to the next year's age). I was VERY ill. It was a day no different than any other day or night. My foster parents were fighting, violently. Innately I had the sense to stay out of their crossfire. But on one particular afternoon, I made the mistake of seeking comfort from a heat register. My right arm was in excruciating pain! By crouching down and pressing my arm against the register, I would find some relief from the warm air blowing from the furnace below. It soothed the dull ache that radiated throughout my right shoulder.

I was too young and innocent to know that a deadly cancer was growing inside me. My foster father would blame me for complaining of the pain, saying I did not eat right. Before I knew what hit me, a vicious slap, then another took me to the floor as I attempted to obey his commands. Barely with enough time to react, I fearfully yielded – hoping he would stop! If I wasn't quick enough for his satisfaction I'd be struck again – with him yelling at me, telling me "he would give me something to cry about if I didn't stop." I usually cried anyway – from the pain in my arm and my heart.

I did not feel I belonged in that home!

Sure enough, I did get a reprieve from the hostility of that home. My foster mother swept me up from the floor as if I was a rag doll. She had the sense to immediately take me to a doctor. From the doctor, I was transported to the hospital.

My distant memory of that hospital was much like that of a scene I read about years later in Aleksandr Solzhenitsyn's book "Cancer Ward." There was peeling pale paint. The room was massive, crowded with wailing children in pre- or post-surgical distress. The odors were memorable as were the sounds and sights of suffering. Not lost on me was the allegorical nature of death around me. Was I, too, dying? I was a witness to death at too early an age, making me wonder of my own mortality. I seriously wondered out loud if anyone left that building alive. The staff and building looked as if they and it were dying.

I remember one of the few visitors being my aunt, who brought me a metallic machine gun toy. It was an early awareness that I had of my left arm adapting for what my right arm could no longer do. I just remember going up and down the halls making a loud rat-a-tat-tat sound! It did not take long to have my new metallic machine gun confiscated by the hospital police.

As the hours waned, my strength did too. I grew weaker and weaker. Though my memory was likely affected by my illness, I honestly cannot recall seeing my parents at my bedside but once or twice. To my foster mom's defense, she also was fighting cancer at the time. My foster father did not believe in cancer. He didn't believe in much but himself.

It was late at night. This, I do vividly recall: A large...okay, I'll say it – FAT doctor came to my bedside, telling me something along the lines of this: "Johnny, it is okay to be scared. You are in a lot of pain. We're going to try to help you. If you wake up tomorrow morning after surgery and have a lot of pain; you still have one arm! If you wake up with no pain, you will be with angels who will take good care of you."

Wow, huh? Indeed, I woke up with the most pain I have ever felt in my life, then or everlastingly. I woke up with my spaghetti-like noodled arm wrapped generously with gauze going around and around my torso. I thought I had one arm, my left. It looked like I did, too. The fact was that the doctors had saved my right arm – and my life! To this day, now knowing the nature of my illness, the odds of my survival baffle my mind.

Unfortunately, the pain did not end. It went on and on, to stalk me viciously at home and school for many years to come. Most the pain was of another kind. To this day, however, it still has its moments with me. Except, now – the arm reminds me of how much Christ suffered for all humanity and that my pain only reminds me it is still attached to my shoulder. When so many have lost limbs defending our country, how can I complain? By the way, when the doctor spoke with me the next day, I gazed out the window, seeing rain pounding the foggy, cracked glass of my prison walls. I quipped, "Nice day to be playing golf, right doc?" Physical therapy followed for many years, often multiple times each week. Never forgotten will be the time a rehab worker placed a golf club in my hands, the idea being that of increasing vascular function in my arm. Without question, this was an early sign of "saving grace" in my young life. It took nearly two years of determination, but eventually, I was able to hold and swing the golf club. Since then, I have deliberately played an annual round of golf in the rain!

It gives me perspective. It is my way of honoring my survival. I have never missed a year! During my teen years, golf became an obsession with me. Eventually, a high school history teacher and coach (for golf and basketball) would figure heavily in my growth and development. Stay tuned, as there is more to come about this wonderful man who became my first father-figure.

The lessons learned from these early memories are that God has us in His protective custody, even when we are suffering and feeling powerless. It also taught me that from an early age to see the glass half full, not empty. We can be grateful for what we still have, not for what we might lose.

It was my first day home from the hospital. I retreated to my area upstairs, a converted attic. The home was a typical 1950's bungalow ranch. My brother, who had the favor of being adopted, had occupancy of the dormer – which happened to have bookshelves flanking both sides of his bed. I was envious of his outside view of the world and those doggone bookshelves. He would also enjoy reading, making him – the older one – most oblivious to the fighting between our parents. He seemed to belong, as if adoptive status suggested greater security.

My biological brother and sister were once part of the Klein household, but parted ways with no explanation. I never knew when my turn to depart would come. I can't say I felt insecure because I would have welcomed a goodbye (though I did have great compassion for my foster mother). She tried hard, but the strain at home showed on her face. She was truly a battered woman, long before I understood the meaning of the word. She and I had that in common – being battered. But, at the time, she and her husband were the only mother and father I knew.

On the first day home from the hospital another occurrence weighed heavily with my memory. My parents argued, not that that in itself was anything new. What I heard was most disturbing. My foster father and mother were arguing over me. What I heard my foster father yell stayed with me for the rest of my life. The pain in my arm was indescribable. Placing it under a pillow comforted the ache. It still does, as subluxations, due to the imbalances and asymmetrical configuration of my right shoulder, remain with me. I had but one pillow.

The physical pain, bad as it was, would have to yield to the psychological pain inflicted on me that day. So, it was my head I buried – to muffle the crying. I wish I was making it up, but I am not. They were arguing over whether to keep me in the home or send me back to foster care services. My foster father, a long-time sympathizer with Nazi Germany – his homeland – screamed "IN GERMANY WE THREW THE G—D--- REJECTS AWAY!"

The old man did not get his way. I thought my foster parents were going to kill each other over me! I buried more than my head and my arm that night. I buried a deep pain that stayed with me for decades to follow. Much later in my adult life, having experienced some sanctification in my faith journey, I was able to exorcise the demons that hijacked my self-esteem. Grace was my guide! One thing was for sure that fateful day: More than ever I knew I did not belong in that home.

Remarkably, one thing my foster parents got right, however, was having me enrolled in catechism classes with the local Roman Catholic Church. For the first time in my young life I learned about God's unconditional love. The teachings of Jesus Christ made sense to my fertile mind and needy spirit. As concepts come and go, prayer was unique: someone I could talk to, if you will (as expressing myself at home was practically forbidden). Prayer captured my imagination, but moreover my heart. I would act out the role of being a priest, by sitting in a closet, holding my little Bible, pretending to conduct Sacraments of Confession, followed by my doling out soft-spoken acts of contrition. No matter my motive, I was having conversations with God. A saving grace? I think so.

Not to get too far ahead of myself here, but suffice to say: later in life I would put that grace into action. Eventually, I'd become my foster father's caregiver for a limited time at the hospital. His wife, at the time, I confess to say was referred to as the "step-monster." She was all talk when it came to support and intentions. Sorry to say, her actions didn't match her words. If ever there was a cover girl for gold diggers, she was it! Before the old man was cold in the ground she helped herself to the entire estate, emptying the house, literally, as the funeral was in process. Not ever expecting any material value from my foster parents, knowing my foster father's delusional wishes were likely for what he perceived as his one and only, it came as no surprise.

My only possession from him is an upholstery hammer (to remember him for the one thing he was good at). When the time came, I eulogized him as an individualist, a natural around animals, flowers and such without mentioning his antipathy for humankind. Yes, it was "grace in action." I flash forward, then back only to illustrate how mysteriously God prepared me to cope and forgive.

A lesson learned from that time was how faith can be more a decision than a debate. My faith journey began with Catholicism, which gave passage to practicing my Christian beliefs with the Baptist, Methodist and Disciples of Christ churches. I've learned that doctrine has its place, but the spirit of the Lord speaks most loudly. More times than I can remember, I've received such grace. And – it shouldn't hurt to be a child. Regularly, I surrendered pain and ill-treatment to the Lord in private prayers, often closeted. I still do.

Just when I thought things couldn't get worse… As a boy, I did not understand much about my illness. My foster mother wanted to show everyone the scar on my arm. I felt like an exhibition at an art show. My foster father didn't want to hear about it or see it. The pain was ever present! Any kind of a bump or backwards motion would transmit excruciating pain down my right arm. Infrequently, on occasion it still does. Nonetheless, I would practice numerous arm, shoulder and hand exercises, to improve range and motion skills. It hurt all the time, but Determination, I decided would be my middle name. In therapy, I learned to give my right arm a "gentle nudge" with my left arm, ever so discreetly and out of notice of those watching me. These miniature actions were needed to aid me in shaking a hand, holding a pencil or lifting to put a cup or plate on a shelf. It occurred to me how graceful the motion became. The notion stuck with me. Today, those I coach good-naturedly tease me about being a man of gentle nudges.

A lifetime of experience has taught me that too often constructive criticism lacks gentleness. Too often people communicate with an attitude of superiority. Or they lack offering anything positive to balance their criticism. When criticism is tendered with personal perspective, such as "I've been there bro…I understand your loss," people are more likely to respond positively if they know their critic has like-experience and empathy – a "gentle spirit," if you will.

As time went by, I would parlay my therapy and exercises into a form of entertainment. One exercise was learning to make my fingers move independently, but in sequence to the other. So I created a comedy routine, featuring my kick-butt impression of Ed Sullivan, the popular host of America's longest running television show of its time. The act was known as "Dancing Fingers," an impersonation of the famous Rockettes or June Taylor Dancers, made famous by The Jackie Gleason Show. Anyway, I would nail Ed Sullivan's squeaky, nasal phrasing. With unnaturally looking raised shoulders and hands on my hips with stiff posturing, I would mimic Mr. Sullivan's oft-quoted "right here on our show (pronounced with great emphasis as shew)…" It made people laugh. I was performing and it made me feel good to see others laugh at my antics.

When I left home years later, my friend Drew nicknamed me Hands (or Kleinhands) because of my dancing fingers. Entertaining others helped me not feel like a reject. It was the embryonic stage of a sense of humor that would become a hallmark to my managing style, parenting skills and coaching methods. American philosopher William James wrote it well: "Common sense and a sense of humor are the same thing, moving at different speeds. A sense of humor is just common sense, dancing." My repertoire included a killer impression of late night *Tonight Show* host Johnny Carson. I also had a not-so-bad parody of a dinosaur host of a family entertainment show aired locally in Cleveland, Ohio called *The Gene Carroll Show*. The amateur performances were pathetic. It featured baton twirlers who barely could walk. Worse were the plaid-shirted, pot-bellied truck drivers – one after another every other week – singing their version of "The Impossible Dream." Lyrically, how apropos. Point is: making others laugh brought me joy.

Laughter, however, did not soothe all my pain. During the 1960's I would experience scores of infections. If it wasn't my ears, it would be my scalp and toes. It mattered not how clean I kept myself. The sores just kept recurring, even requiring a tube to be inserted in my neck to drain puss. It was gross. I felt like Frankenstein. My foster father would pierce the boils and carbuncles with hot needles, not showing an ounce of compassion – just telling me to "shut up!" You guessed it: Or, he would give me something to cry about. I learned to bury the pain.

My middle name wasn't actually Determination. It was Joseph. That name never caused me any issues, but my last name did. Until the tenth grade – for whatever reason – I was mandated to place on every school assignment and document both my biologically given name and that of my foster parents. So, at times I'd write John J. Klein (McHue) and at other times John J. McHue (Klein). Weird, right? How that didn't cause me an identity crisis I'll never know, but it did cause me much teasing. Classmates can be cruel. The teasers would call me McCutey. It - they - got to me. I would let the hurt show, which made it worse. They made me feel different, mocked and embarrassed; thus, it made me angry!

Good or bad, pain or laughter, my identity was shaping one way or the other. Pain comes in many forms. Antibiotics had become a way of life for me, given my immunity issues. But there was no medicine I enjoyed more every month than that which I read faithfully in each month's publication of Reader's Digest. It was called "Laughter is the Best Medicine." By God's grace, my pathway became one where humor won over the anguish.

A lesson learned was that God reveals joy, even when we suffer pain. Laughter, indeed, is the best medicine. I didn't understand it during my childhood, but having an audience became part of knowing my own identity – which, in some mystical way, became my pathway to a victory march. Someone once wrote, "When you find your audience, you find yourself." In coaching I encourage others to realize how important it is to not let anyone else define their own identity.

MIDDLE SCHOOL

Middle school, or junior high as some might call it, should be a time for young adolescents to explore their uniqueness through learning structures that encourage independent means. For most in the 1960's it was a transitional time, whereby educational programs would foster growth and welcome change in the life and ambitions of a young person at the doorstep of the adult world. Solon, Ohio schools aspired excellence in education in every sense of the word. The commercial and residential economic development of this southeastern suburb of Cleveland was well-planned by community designers, making our district one of the finest in the country. I benefited greatly from the high school education I had; but – middle school was another matter.

My stature, self-image and reputation made me the target of many bullies. Likely, I was the source of bewilderment for more than a few teachers. I was hot-tempered. Today, I'm slow to anger. But, in the middle school years the rage and resentment at home was growing inside me.

By the age of thirteen and fourteen my right shoulder (quadrant) was significantly smaller, asymmetrical and sloped (off axis, tilting) as opposed to the left side of me. It drew attention, no matter how I carried myself. Plus, protecting the arm was priority. Any little bump, from a crowded hallway between classes, contact in gym class or something as simple as gravity, would cause partial dislocation of my arm and shoulder (subluxations).

To this day, the pain occasionally revisits me. And it is unique to other kinds of pain. Many times I would just ride the pain out. As I pursued my interest in golf, pain became a constant companion with just about any swing. I played anyway, determined that my arm was not going to stop me from playing golf. Any kind of motion had an effect on it. Just recently when vacationing at Disneyland a friend helped me overcome my fear of roller-coasters, because for years I'd avoid them, knowing sudden twists and turns might provoke distress. Doctors, having a penchant for scaring me with their warnings, gave me reason to limit myself, over-protecting my arm. Constantly, I would have trepidation that someone or something was going to bring harm to my arm. Oh, if only I had the friends I have now when being bullied in school so many years ago. The teasing was cruel and relentless. And the pain – emotional and physical - just never went away. I just felt alone in this world. I was a nomad drifting between classes with indifferent students and teachers. I might as well have been a zombie.

My two companions were pain and books. Books had enduring power to my brain, though. Innately, I wanted more out of life, but rage and resentment kept building inside me, both hijacking the happiness I so desired. Thank God, the books I read fed my determination when reading about "mind over matter." So, I embraced the pain, allowing it to fuel my love affair with the golf swing. It was a strange time in my life. The resentment I felt and combated at home extended itself to school. Knowing how to gain acceptance at home or school was foreign to me.

Books - being my friends - created a curiosity with libraries for me. They fascinated me. Libraries were safe haven for me to read about heroes (biographies), one being Andrew Carnegie. Reading about men and women who overcame great odds gave me hope. I had a wistful bias for Mr. Carnegie because he was Scottish-American. After all, I knew my bloodline had Scottish origins. And the man was a rags to riches success story. I suspect, when reading about him as a boy, it was the onset of my becoming a dreamer. It is no wonder that the creations of Walt Disney would capture my imagination (as well as the whole world).

Meantime, life was hard! I needed speech classes to correct phonetic and articulation issues, likely caused from both my cancer and family history. Several years later, when of majority age, I would learn of an abnormal cleft palate, which would require several oral surgeries, further aggravated by a misfitted mouthpiece worn with braces. It also played a role with numerous ear infections. It was difficult to chew food. The pain, so evident to others around me - especially when eating lunch - drew unwanted attention resulting in more taunting. It is one thing to be a whiner; it's another thing to actually be in pain. The pain, in all its forms, was very real to me during those critical years of childhood development. It made me feel inferior to others (Mr. Reject). I hated how others made fun of me. It was never more prominent than during a seventh-grade physical education class, when an extremely well-developed boy with the physique of a high school athlete was literally put on display by the gym teacher. I was next to him. It was as if we were in some body-building program of "before and after." Of course, I saw myself, believing that's how others saw me too, as the "before" model. This was an era when Charles Atlas (known for his landmark advertising methods on bodybuilding) was in every comic book, depicting a ninety-nine pound weakling getting sand kicked in his face. That would be me. Today it is a funny memory. Back then it was more fodder for all the thirteen year old comedians that perceived themselves as future bodybuilders.

God, however, was in control. As tough an era the middle school years were, it was an incredible time of Camelot. America had great potential and promise. John F. Kennedy was president. America loved him! He was Catholic, which made my foster parents and many more in our very Catholic community happy. President Kennedy was charming, possessing glamorous speaking skill, especially when displaying deft wit with the press corps. The president and another charming and popular fellow, golfing legend Arnold Palmer, had something their contemporaries did not. It was charisma. They coined the word. These two media darlings of the coming of age television era had phenomenal impact on an entire generation. Being of that generation, I was particularly drawn to their personalities and leadership. Kennedy was smart and courageous. Palmer was strong and popular. I wanted to be like them. There were others that roused my interest, like Johnny Carson, the long-standing host of *The Tonight Show*. I read how much of his success was due to his philosophy "to never make a guest look bad." That philosophy became part and parcel of my own philosophy later in life.

Also, Frank Sinatra was making a comeback (making music, not noise). I wanted to command a stage like him. Walt Disney and his weekly television program would provide an hour of reprieve from the chaos in the Klein household (not to mention it feeding the dreamer in me). Later, I read how Mr. Disney called his staff "Imagineers." I wanted to be an Imagineer!

The men described in the last paragraph were my heroes, at least those known to all America. They would become role models for me, greatly shaping my personal philosophy and "guiding principles" for life.

All that shaping of character would come later. Meanwhile, life was still hard.

The constant bullying at home and school made me withdraw that much more to my books and into a strange new hobby of collecting old antique typewriters and topically anomalous encyclopedias. Learning was an adventure for me. So, when seeing the word "heuristic," I immediately identified with its meaning. Encouragement was already being programmed into my child mind. Typing was great therapy for my right arm, when not entertaining my friends with dancing fingers. I would type for hours, transcribing whatever I might be reading at the time. It was just fun. And I felt I was getting smarter, but in a very unconventional manner. I would use this old red typing textbook bought from a rummage sale to test my speed and accuracy. I was in my own world. The encyclopedias were something else. They were offbeat subjects, like the "Papers of the Presidents."

It amazed me what a comprehensive collection of more than a dozen books could reveal in the president's own words. It was like eavesdropping on their private conversations, which just happened to become public policy. Equally amazing was how many of these seemingly rare encyclopedic reference resources could be found in flea markets. Later I will share with you a very special relationship with a history teacher during my high school days. The intense interest that would later develop with American History was undoubtedly conceived from these early experiences with books and typewriters. I was doing book reports before they were assigned. And I was a writer before I knew what a writer was. God was way ahead of me.

During my early teens some of my favorite books included The *Hardy Boys* series, created by Edward Stratemeyer, founder of a book-packaging firm. The detective series featured two brave and adventurous brothers capable of solving mysteries. They had ideal boyhood manners and keen deductive skills. They would make good overcome evil. I liked that idea, given my frame of reference at home. *Old Man and the Sea* by Ernest Hemingway (also brilliantly portrayed in the movie version by Spencer Tracy) was a story of a man alone, trying to feed his community as a down on his luck fisherman. It impressed me how the authors and actors sold the scene: a man alone at sea – period! There was also Earl Stanley Gardner, who inspired the long-running television series called *Perry Mason*. The books and shows featured a very ethical lawyer who just never lost a case. He was a winner. And he was kind and generous, one who excelled in his field. Lord knows, I could have used his services later in my life.

All these heroes and books would become bookends to shaping my identity and character.

Before there would be gains, more pain was on the horizon. During my middle school years there would be an unexpected surprise, one that would bring me hope and a sense of brotherhood (love and acceptance), only to be recalled, ending in sorrow and personal loss.

One day a car pulled into our driveway. Two young boys would exit the car with suitcases in hand. Curiously, the Klein's had taken in two more foster children! They had already adopted Richard, as I indicated earlier. Richard just liked being to himself. We never disliked one another. We just had separate lives when growing up in Solon, Ohio.

My foster father and he had an altogether different relationship than what I had with the old man. He was closer to my foster father, having an interest in cars, guns and scouts. He was not a reject. Joey and Mike were the newcomers and were closer to my own age. Immediately a chemistry existed between Mike and myself. He would sleep in the bed next to me, laughing late into the night, swapping jokes and arm-wrestling (left arms only) with me. Joey was withdrawn, preferring company to himself. But, Mike and I would go hiking, eat together and throw baseballs. He'd be thoughtfully patient with me as I caught with my left arm, then with a well self-taught motion, slip my mitt off and throw with the same left arm. I got pretty good at it. We used to walk better than two miles to the middle school that had summer craft programs. We'd construct miniature bridges and block houses out of ice cream sticks. I'd do what I could as Mike would do more of the detail work that my right arm and hand didn't do as well at. We were a team! We were foster brothers. We would share sodas and milk shakes when walking home. He made me feel loved and accepted just as I was, just as I did him.

Just as quickly as Joey and Mike appeared on the scene, they just as suddenly left! It was shocking. With no advanced notice, "the car" arrived in our driveway to take them away. My foster parents prohibited me from saying goodbye. No handshakes. No hugs. No explanations. I was allowed to wave goodbye. I never saw or heard from them again. The pain was great as ever! This time it was more than my arm. It was my heart.

As tough as the seventh and eighth grades were, the ninth grade assigned me to a biology teacher who ran the audio-visual program at the high school. He was also a freshman basketball coach. I had an interest in biology because I wanted to know more about my own health. I tried to play freshman basketball, but it was a disaster. Every time I got bumped or shoved I practically went into convulsions on the gym floor. Worse, I'd start to cry, feeling so inferior to other kids. They could do everything I wanted to be. Coach Moran, however, took me under his wing, introducing me to Coaches Belich and Duffner, coaches for the junior varsity and varsity, respectfully. These men would eventually become added to my collection of heroes. They were my first father-figures. I felt like a mascot. The coaching staff took a liking to me. That was an uncommon feeling for me. They showed me the absolute fundamentals (old school) on how to shoot a basketball – LEFT HANDED! Over the next three years, excuse me for boasting – I would learn to shoot so proficiently NO ONE would beat me in a game of H-O-R-S-E. Once, I remember making forty-three foul shots in a row. But, that's a story to be told for the high school years.

My biology teacher decided I'd make a good volunteer with taking audio-visual equipment where needed in the school. It was my first taste of being given responsibility. It was fun. Later, I'd be the guy at the local community theater showing classic films on Saturday afternoons. I had a part-time job!

The genesis from my boyhood through middle school years might suggest that my life was nothing but pain. While out of the ordinary, it was the only life I knew. And my parents, for better or worse were the only mother and father I knew. When trying to survive a hostile environment one becomes a bit accustomed to it. Knowing your parents would argue continuously became a matter of expectation. I would insulate my mind from their yelling, choosing to ignore them, yet hoping it might get better one day. It never did. Having said that, they were incredible actors! They'd charm friends when visiting, acting like everything was fine inside their pretentious version of Camelot. I'd be coached what to say and not say before company arrived. To the outside world all seemed well in paradise.

Notwithstanding the charade at home, the health challenges and anger growing within me were atoned somewhat by the heroes appearing on my mental radar screen. Sadly, some heroes succumbed to a cruel and tragic fate. John F. and Robert F. Kennedy had their lives (and ours) robbed by bullets, as did Martin Luther King. All those men were so eloquent. They were great leaders! I have more to say about them in later chapters, but suffice to say for now that these men, regardless of one's party affiliation, had characteristics that showed greatness! As life was beating me up, I was paying attention to their messages and the way they could work a crowd. As author John C. Maxwell writes, they more than communicated, they connected with their audiences.

While coping with the chaos inside the walls at Aurora Road, Solon, Ohio, my attention was less on that of my parents and more on the leaders of that time. Not belonging, in many ways, seemed like not all together a bad thing. Many years later, when in leadership roles, it became very apparent to me that many others would relate to my plight. For the 1960's were turbulent, if ever there was an understatement. Later, other than assassinations, there would be an ill-fated war, politically called The Vietnam Conflict, a disgraced president resigning, racial strife, Woodstock, which showcased from a muddy field in New York a shock culture and psychedelic behavior that did not connect with me.

Certain teachers showed an interest in me. Some classmates found my antics amusing. And my foster parents had bought a farm in rural Pennsylvania to restore (next chapter). All in all, my life was no less turbulent than the times I lived in.

Lessons were learned from these painful years, although seeded by some modest developments. Not unlike the "weeping prophet" Jeremiah, I'd be called in my youth to intrinsically sense leadership, though many of my peers would underestimate me or not take notice. But, like Jeremiah, God calls us…guides us – often without us understanding it, to be 'positive' in negative times. I had not yet known Jesus in a 'personal' way; yet, His truths were revealed to me. Heroes surfaced, with me emulating their styles. I still didn't belong, but I knew my life was heading somewhere better. Years before actually joining the Noon Day Optimist Club, I was an optimist by nature.

HIGH SCHOOL

1966 was a year when a gathering storm was building for all of America, if not the world. Racial relations were worsening, President Johnson was preoccupied with his Great Society programs, sadly fumbling the Vietnam Conflict, which was escalating into a disastrous war (one that scars this nation to this day). Postage stamps were only five cents. Star Trek beamed itself into our television viewing scene. Truman Capote wrote a blockbuster book entitled *In Cold Blood*. One of my heroes, Frank Sinatra, was crooning about the September of His Years. I couldn't get enough of watching the Boston Celtics whip their opponents in professional basketball.

I wanted to shoot baskets every spare moment of my life. I was good at it! And Christopher Plummer and Julie Andrews starred in one of the greatest films made, *The Sound of Music* (nominated for Best Picture). Oh, how I loved to listen to the benediction-like lyrics of *Edelweiss*: "May the Lord, mighty God, bless and keep you forever…Grant you peace, perfect peace, courage in every endeavor. Lift your eyes to see His face, and His grace forever…May the Lord, mighty God, bless and keep you forever."

By this time I was a precocious teenager, mentally anyway. Emotionally, I was not. Physically – not even a close call. My body was underdeveloped. Surviving the hostility at home only got worse. But, mentally, I knew I was smart (not as dumb as my foster father insisted I was) because I was very well read. Being informed felt like a prize to me. Having said that, however, I still lacked confidence. When we lack confidence, we are not emotionally equipped to deal with difficult people or situations (Years later I would read many of Dr. Robert Schuller's *Possibility Thinking* books, which were inspired by his mentor, Dr. Norman Vincent Peale, author of *The Power of Positive Thinking*.

Being smart seemed pointless if no one accepted or respected you for it. My older adopted brother was in college. My foster parents practically had him destined as the leader of the free world. With him gone from the home, it was open season for the old man to take his anger out on his wife and me. I sincerely wish this was a figment of my imagination; however – it's nothing but the truth: I cannot remember a solitary night when my foster parents did not violently fight with one another. God forbid if I entered the fray. And – for whatever reason, many of their arguments centered on me. It was hard to not take such personally. It made for one very sensitive young man. For years that became a liability. With maturity, grace and a lifetime's perspective and as an encourager, it is now an asset, one which enables me to be tuned into another person's innermost struggle. When others kindly speak of me as having a "knack" for understanding others, it is because I remained "sensitive" - but did so with a sanctifying spirit.

Time and again, I'd retreat to my books and music. *Edelweiss* intrigued me, my never getting enough of the song and its lyrics. Same with Frank Sinatra and Perry Como. I admired the delivery and passion they both poured into their music. The songs always told a story, usually – with strong feeling - about love. I believe that grace is part of our language of love, which gets beautifully expressed through the sounds of music. The Catholic Church had taught me early on that grace was an undeserved help as our God called us to be children of God. Of course, the theologians gave us discourse on the scholarly aspects and history of grace; but, for me, grace was simple. Giving it just came naturally for me. I found it easier to forgive those "who trespass against us," than to debate those "who have no heart for the truth (Proverbs)." I abhorred conflict. I heard enough of it every night at home. But, conflict would dog me for many years. Indeed, God prepared me well (as you will see when reading what radio broadcaster, Paul Harvey used to call, "the rest of the story.") There was a reason for much of that conflict, but I wasn't buying it as a young fellow. As an older gentleman, I've learned that life was and is a university. We can choose to be or not be in attendance. For those of us who pay attention to what life teaches us, the next challenge is to apply what we learned the next time we are faced with a similar situation.

Given the home environment and lack of self-confidence, for some inexplicable reason my curiosity made me wanting for knowledge. Speculation today would have me believe it had more to do with   the environment of my school. While bullies often had their way with me in middle school, high school was a passage, giving way to people that reached out to me. It was grace in action. One teacher taught "clear-thinking principles." The lessons on problem-solving served me well the rest of my life. I loved learning how to be principled, logical and objective. We'd study how to set biases and prejudices aside. When handling a conflict, finding subordinate points of agreement was critical to establishing common goals. Separating emotion from the good judgment made sense to me. Recognizing that one's opponent might actually be right became an exercise in humility and logic. When at the library, genres on history piqued more of my curiosity because the inevitably it would involve conflicts.

Conflicts involved people. And people and their conflicts made for stories about resolutions, often in the form of biographies, whether they be about the good, bad or ugly. Whether looking for it or not, grace was shown to me by one of the finest men I've ever known. His name was Mr. Clarence Duffner. He was an American History teacher at Solon High School. He also coached varsity basketball and golf, as mentioned briefly, earlier in this book. He was a large man and very passionate in his teaching and coaching. He was also the only man I ever witnessed standing up to my foster father. I had come to school one day pretty banged up. I tried to shy away from talking about it, but "coach" wouldn't let it go. He wanted to know what happened to me. I eventually broke down. Coach Duffner took me home after school, telling me to stand to the side as he approached my foster father in the back yard. I was scared to death! I heard coach say, "If that boy ever shows up at school like this again, you will have to deal with me!" I was scared spitless! I literally thought my life might be over. Incredibly, the old man never said a word to me. I went to bed that night, as usual hearing he and my mom fight. I don't remember why.

I no longer cared why or what they quarreled over. I'd drown them out with my radio. And always, there were my books. Thank God! Don't ask me why, but I just felt compelled to keep writing, transcribing and even penning lyrics to songs that had no meter or arrangement. It was just intuitive. It was also therapeutic.

I couldn't get enough of American History and basketball. I was hooked. Mr. Duffner and his coaching staff had encouraged me to keep reading – while also learning how to shoot baskets. Not just in any ordinary way, but how to excel at it better than anyone in the entire school. It was if they got together and made a goal amongst themselves, saying something like, let's see what great things we can do with this kid. The attention and time they gave me was something unfamiliar to me.

In a year's time, I had a reputation as the kid who could beat anyone in a basketball game called H-O-R-S-E. I'd line my pockets with quarters, shooting baskets at any opportunity before, during or after school. If it wasn't chump change, it was for bowls of tomato soup (when the cafeteria had it on the menu). Safe bet to say I like cream of tomato soup. I even beat the great Jim Mandich (at HORSE, of course), who went on to play as tight end for Don Shula's undefeated 1972 Miami Dolphins football team.

Coach Duffner made me the manager of the varsity basketball team. It empowered me, as he depended on me to be accurate as a statistician. I would sit next to him during games. During games he would lean into me and talk to me as if I was an assistant coach. Without ever posturing a false sense of importance, I grew exponentially as my responsibilities expanded. On game days, we wore suits. I liked the way I felt and looked. My self-esteem was better and I felt like I belonged.

The coaches decided that my shooting skills could be tapped to teach freshman players. They also wanted me to work with young middle school kids on Saturdays. So, they actually started calling me, rather informally, assistant shooting coach for the freshman team, coached by Mr. Moran (my biology teacher). I would recite precisely word-for-word what my coaches taught me. The freshman kids listened because I could actually demonstrate what I told them. Words can be persuasive, but actions have a way of driving a point home. I never forgot that simple truth.

A most memorable occasion was the District Championship being played at Bedford High School. As manager, I would join the team for warm-ups, shooting baskets just as if I, too, was an athlete/player. On that occasion – forgive my boasting – I was killing it (as we say now). Everything I put up with my left arm went through the hoop! SWISH! SWOOSH! SWISH! One after another. It mattered not where I shot from: From the corners (slightly behind the board), foul line, top of the key and so on. Never will I forget that moment. I overheard the coaches talking from the sidelines.

Cleveland East Tech was notoriously known for their state-bound championships. In other words, they were nearly unbeatable. Basically, the opposing team's coach declared, "HOLY COW! Who the heck is that kid? What a weapon!" Coach Duffner quipped, "Oh, that's just our manager." To this day that fond memory makes me chuckle, just as it did that night. For one brief moment, I was a threat to the opposition! In other words, if you think he's something, wait till you see the rest of the team play. For the record, our Solon Comets lost.

Fond as that memory was, there was great disappointment and pain associated with it. Before I enjoyed the aforementioned attention and opportunity to develop in leadership, I had to ride out what had become an inevitable flash of rejection. A couple months before being designated a rather unusual kind of team manager I had to grapple with the coach's decision to cut me from the team. He directed me to his office, telling me to literally take a seat on top of his desk and wait for me. He had tears in his eyes, saying "Johnny, I must cut you from the squad." It was gut-wrenching! Naturally, "reject" came to mind. I never wanted anything – at that time of my life – more than to be on the varsity basketball team. He went out to the gym where he assembled both the varsity and junior varsity teams. He told them that if anyone had half my desire to play, the Solon Comets would be one great team – that no one would beat us!

The coach returned to console me, explaining my "physical limitations" (arm/health status) and the "risk" associated with injury (liability and likelihood of injury). He then told me I'd make a GREAT manager!" Little did I know how developmental that would become later in my corporate life. It was fundamental to leadership roles that would come my way years later.

When not shooting baskets I was putting golf balls, reading and giving a GAZILLION book reports to my father-figure, coach, and history teacher – Mr. Duffner. I'd put the poor guy asleep, asking for extra credit. I would give him book reports weekly. The man had the patience of Job. He had the heart of Christ. I loved that man! I would take a bullet for him. Later, he would become an early recipient of an annual Thanksgiving tradition of mine: To write a letter to someone thanking them for making my life better. I have written an annual letter of gratitude at Thanksgiving for forty-seven years and counting.

As fate would have it, Coach Duffner would try me out for the golf team (liability and injury were not the same obstacle as other sports). My skills were marginal, but the "desire" and "determination" traits got me a spot on the team. One thing I could do very, very well was putt! Just like shooting baskets. I putted like a "bandit," as my neighborhood buddy Dennis would say. Putting became as profitable as shooting baskets. I never lacked a reservoir of quarters. I still have the vintage Wilson Hol-Hi putter, rust spotted and wrapped with tape. It is a keepsake…a treasure.

It was very early in the morning when I received an unexpected phone call from my golf coach, telling me a team member, Billy, had taken ill and could not play in the conference golf championship. They NEEDED me to play or our team would be forced to forfeit. A cold drizzle put a damper on the event. But, we played.

No one knew that the cold temperatures and damp weather would be a worst-case scenario for me. Vascular function in my right arm was not and still is not very efficient in cold weather. Being grateful for the chance to participate and knowing how important it was that I finish, I didn't want anyone to know that I had, for all intents and purposes, lost feeling in my arm. It literally turned dark blue, if not nearly purple. On practically every swing I experienced a subluxation. No matter what I did to hide it from my opponent, it was impossible to keep him from seeing my demise.

The other player told his coach about my condition when we finished the front nine, which forced me to stop playing, resulting in – you guessed it – forfeit! My coach took me to the hospital for treatment. My foster father scolded me with an "I told you so." Had I not had what some call a disability, I imagine I might have been a fierce competitor had I been more physically gifted. One thing was for sure: I didn't lack desire and determination. For years I'd be told by doctors to be more satisfied with mediocrity. Somerset Maugham wrote, "Only mediocre people are at their best." I wanted to get better at everything I did. So, if so-called experts wanted to call me an overachiever, so be it. I always wanted to exceed expectations!

Due to changes in equipment, philosophies with physical therapy/conditioning and the evolution of the golf ball, I've learned to play better at an age when people retire than what I could do when a young man. Not vane, just sane. I'm a reasoned man. If you don't let other people define your capability and strive to use what is left, not what is taken from you, it is astonishing how the human body and an active imagination can compensate for re-sectioned muscles. As agonizing as it was to cause my team to forfeit a victory, the character development was well worthwhile. I was not a quitter. And I put my team first. It mattered when I was seventeen years old and it matters today.

A Victory March

Middle school and high school were just really tough years, for all the reasons cited in my story. Yet, strides were being made with overcoming my inferiority complex. Having audio-visual responsibilities (modest as they were) and being a manager for the basketball team was huge to my personal growth.

Excelling in Mr. Duffner's American History class, however, would become one of my proudest accomplishments. One day, during finals, Mr. Duffner scolded the class for being ill-prepared – except for my performance. To be honest, it was embarrassing. I expected classmates to shun me, thinking I was some kind of teacher's pet. Perhaps I was to some degree, but no one gave me a hard time over it. Mr. Duffner nominated me for a Kiwanis (Civic Organization) Award, for "Outstanding Achievement in the Field of History." I was awarded a beautiful plague and given a dinner of recognition. My foster parents did not attend.

For the first time in my young life I received public recognition for being the best at something! I dreamed of going to college, seeking higher learning – like my brother (still destined to be the leader of the free world…and likely more). Surely, becoming a senior would cap my high school years. How wrong I was.

1967 was graduation year for this young Solon Comet, but not before unspeakable tragedy would befall our school and community. Just as movie producers like to set a scene, it was a dark and stormy night. I was finding refuge from the foster home, where I left my parents behind to argue and drink. Friends just down the street knew of my living conditions and made their home mine too. They had a large family. What was one more kid? I got along with everyone in the family, especially when Mrs. Leslie would make her angel hair spaghetti. It was like a prize meal from the county fair. Their home was a popular place for many from our school to hang out at.

Such was the case one late night while a bunch of us flopped over furniture or took a spot on the floor to watch a late-night horror host named Ghoulardi. His devilish antics of mayhem and mockery made for adolescent non-stop laughing. Suddenly there was a sickening squeal of rubber burning and an engine sound piercing the night air. A couple classmates had just left the house. In a second, it was evident to us: it was the sounds of glass shattering and metal crushing! I would bruise my head on an end table, instinctively running for the telephone to call the police. Without doubt, an awful accident had just occurred, shattering lives as well. The life of one of our talented classmates was taken from us – and his family! In a split second Phil was gone forever. Unless you've never been a party to such a tragic scene, there are no words to describe the pain and suffering. My friends down the street had more history and fellowship with Phil, but the day I sat on Phil's bed – after his death and burial – talking with and consoling his mother and father is unforgettable.

Not long afterwards I was hit head-on by a driver who came through a red light at the main intersection of our suburb. I was waiting to turn left with an arrow. There was nowhere to go. Reality hit me hard! My knees, left arm and sternum took the worse of it. While being transported to the hospital by ambulance with the other driver, I was told by him, "Gee kid, I'm so sorry!" Later he recanted his story (perhaps after sobering up). The cars were a mess. The impact put the engine practically in my lap. The back axle had snapped, so I was told. In any event, I was trapped in the car, but fortunately was a few hundred feet from the fire station. Incredibly, a family friend's brother went to my foster parents' front door, advising them of the accident, while also speculating that I might be "dead." Kids! Unbelievable, right? I was apparently unconscious for a short while and my friend's brother saw me on his way home, making a rash assumption.

Now – get this! Talk about unbelievable. My foster father – and I am not making this up, as Dave Barry, the satirical writer would say – went to the junk yard to see the car before coming to the hospital! If that doesn't make you feel unimportant, I don't know what would. From the moment the old man saw me at the hospital, until late that night upon release – looking like a black and blue punching bag, not to mention the shock – he did nothing but SCREAM at me! He was ticked! After all, the car was badly damaged. I wanted to die. It dawned on me that surviving cancer was not much different than surviving life (that line would come back to me in my adult life when asked to give a speech to the Relay for Life organization. I share more about that experience further into the book).

Thank God, I did graduate. For reasons I'd prefer to keep private, my helping a friend was noticed by his uncle who happened to be a bank executive in downtown Cleveland, Ohio. He and his social worker wife had some insights about my family situation and wanted to help. He told me when graduating, "Come see me at the bank and we'll see what we can do for you." Banking became my profession of first choice.

I loved it! And I was grateful. Yes, a few short years later, Mr. Wilson became a recipient of one of my annual Thanksgiving Tribute letters.

1967 was moving towards 1968 – a year in American History to not be forgotten!

For the first time I really felt I belonged.

Lessons learned were many. While I had not yet accepted Christ as my personal Savior, it was apparent that God had a plan for my life…And that, indeed – there was a God. While life was tough, especially at home, there were opportunities abound. It seemed like "good people" would come into my life just when I thought no one cared. In contrast to the brokenness I experienced at home, I began to see how other families behaved. Hard work, I could now see, did yield recognition and opportunity. Reaping what we sow made sense to me. My reading habits became voracious, constantly yearning to be informed. Definitely, I learned that it pays to be informed.

WORLD OF WORK: ROOKIE YEAR

It was 1968 and I had already graduated the year before from high school, taking up the offer of my friend's uncle, who worked at the bank. The banking world was in concert with all that I learned about in American History. The American Institute of Banking had coursework available for continuing education credits. I ate them up.

Later, when chief operating officer for an affiliate bank I would use my course material as part of an orientation program to make new employees better identify with their chosen field. Back then, unlike current corporate trends to do more with less, I would get all the overtime I desired. I'd work insane hours, to make money and to create opportunities for recognition and advancement.

Now and then, I would sprint home from work, leaving just enough time for a few holes of golf at Grantwood Golf Course, located at the corners of Aurora Road and Pettibone Road, in Solon, Ohio. My buddies and I would meet up and play "skin games." I was still using my Wilson putter. My putting style at that time was like that of Arnold Palmer, taught to me by Grange Alves, a man who looked remarkably like professional golfer *Julius Boros*. Knowing of my arm subluxations – even from gravity – he showed me how to wrist putt like Arnie, resting my right elbow on my right hip. What others could do with their long irons and woods, I would make up for on the putting green.

Grantwood Golf Course has special memories for me, not just for usually getting beat there, but because it is where I met some of the best friends a guy could ever hope to have in life. Bobby Z. was employed part-time at the course. Often we would pass by one another while on our way to work in the mornings. He was always talking up classic movies and great Broadway shows, especially the Sound of Music. That made for an instant likability factor between us. He, more than most, treated me rather kindly, particularly showing compassion (not pity) for my arm issues. He related to my life at home. As the years went by we would involve one another in our weddings. We remain close. He's like a brother to me. His wife, Joy, lives up to her name. Later, when married, my wife and I would have some great laughs with them as couples. Bob is also my insurance man!

Another friend I met at Grantwood Golf Course was Drew. To this day he would play it down, but it was Drew that first gave me the courage to move out of my parent's home. He lived in an apartment with his parents on Northfield Road. The location made for a closer commute to downtown Cleveland. The idea of leaving my foster mom in the hands of my foster dad frightened me. She'd been suffering from the effects of cancer for years. My foster father's indifference to her plight – not to mention their dislike for each other – gave me some guilt, as if I was abandoning my mother (leaving her to fend for herself). Drew reminded me that she (my foster mother) made that choice: to stay with him. Call it battered wife syndrome or whatever, he was right. It was time for me to move on.

1968 was a watershed year for America. It was a watershed year for me too. I was lying in bed, still at home in Solon, listening to the radio late at night. Naturally, my foster parents were arguing. Suddenly, there was breaking news! Robert F. Kennedy had been shot, while campaigning in Los Angeles, California at the Ambassador Hotel. For a brief moment, while at work on my lunch hour, I got to stand near his limousine as it passed by. His enthusiasm and intelligence was unmistakable. He was a leader! Lord, could he speak with passion. His off the cuff comments on the night of Martin Luther King's assassination were so heartfelt and poignant. RFK appeared in a poor neighborhood of Indianapolis, having heard the awful news.

He told the mostly black crowd, "For those of you who are black and are tempted… to be filled with hatred and mistrust of the injustice of such an act, against all white people, I would only say that I can also feel in my own heart the same kind of feeling," He went on, saying "I had a member of my family killed…he was killed by a white man."

While other cities rioted that night, Indianapolis did not! Robert F. Kennedy was the real deal. Hearing of his assassination made me cry. His book, To *Seek A Newer World* was a favorite of mine because it offered hope through reasoned solutions, compassion and reconciliation. Books, not bullets could make the world a better place.

The time had come for me to move into an apartment, just above my buddy Drew's place. We would shag golf balls for hours behind Chanel High School (where both my other buddies Dave and Bob had attended the parochial Catholic school), where we would have some guilt when bouncing a ball or two off the Mother Mary statue. Not long afterwards, two more friends, Billy and Bob (not Billy Bob) moved into the complex. My bachelor pad became a central hangout, making my friends feel that much more like family to me. My foster father told me that I might as well have moved to the other side of the planet. He was bitter at me for "abandoning" my foster mother. No kidding.

So, 1968, was, indeed, a watershed year; it was pivotal for me personally and professionally. My banking job was affording me considerable opportunity to learn and gain responsibility. The long commute, together with constant tension at home was forcing my decision to break away.

By this time readers might get the impression that I had developed a constant resentment, contempt and willful discontent towards my foster father, no matter what he said or did. Such a presumption could not be farther from the truth and my wishes. Throughout my childhood, extending into adulthood, I would call my foster father "dad, father or pop." Often, I would tell him and my mom that I loved them. It was my nature to do so. Each time I would wait for an echo. It never came. Unbelievably, not once in my upbringing can I remember either of them saying "I love you (too)." Not once was I ever introduced as their son! It was always "Johnny." Perhaps I expected too much.

I loved them anyway.

Grace was not something I questioned. Simply, I accepted it…embraced it. As my spiritual awakening evolved, I believed it was part of my design by God. Grace would become a cornerstone word for my personhood. Later in life, the other cornerstone word would be "encourager."

Just before I made the big "move" a neighborhood friend of mine, Dennis, and I decided to seek some spirituality in our lives. We began attending a small Nazarene church in nearby Bedford. When not being mischievous with one another, we would actually listen to the sermons and attend Sunday school classes together. We even played a little basketball with the church team. Long story short, I surrendered my life and soul, wanting a personal relationship with Christ. Wisest decision I ever made.

Today, I call myself a bit of a rogue Christian. I still attend church, but not as regularly. And I am, of course, a Believer! However, after numerous roles with the organized church though the decades, I've grown somewhat sour with how the "business of the church" is conducted. I am also disappointed with how many ministers and lay leaders cleverly and subtly work political agendas into their services and sermons. Tenets and doctrine should have a place in a house of worship, but personal and political agendas should not!

The teachings of Christ take precedent for me. My experience has shown me that Christ-like characteristics get pushed to the back burner when and where the business of the church is involved. Many years ago a pastor friend of mine explained it well: "Church is not a resting home for saints; it's a hospital for sinners," he said. I always liked that description, when considering the proper behavior of a church family.

So it was. I moved on, leaving in my wake a battered woman, yet a brave new world of independence ahead for me. My education continued, but now I belonged to the world of work. No more probation on the new job. A banker was I! I wore three-piece suits and my friends fondly called me "The Banker." I had an identity.

Lesson learned was that grace was given freely. It didn't need to be earned. That lesson was the key to my personal and spiritual growth. Understanding that there was a "Father of all fathers" gave me hope that one day I would make a good father (and that I would do it much differently than the example shown me). The Lord's Prayer meant more than ever to me ("Our Father who art in Heaven…"). A victory march had begun.

WORLD OF WORK: GROWING PAINS AND GAINS

Anybody that has ever worked in operations knows of the time pressures and deadlines that go with the job. It is a labor-intensive environment. In banking, during the 1970's, titles were taken seriously, just one step from a para-military operation. When delivering and servicing financial products, customer service expectations were high. People were demanding when it came to handling their money. As our customer base grew exponentially, so did the expectations with staff. Constantly, there was more to do all the time.

Our bank was a leader in introducing new and competitive financial products. I was eager to understand, service and train others on them. There was much to know and learn, at times making it all feel a bit overwhelming. Likewise, there was much I did not know. The trick was for me was to better understand what I was reading about regarding Plato: What do I know? What do I not know? And, what do I need to know that I don't know? I knew I didn't have to know everything. Yet, long before Google was on the scene, I needed to get better at brokering information. Doing so is both a science and an art. Former Secretary of State, Donald Rumsfeld subscribed many of Plato's early and scholarly beliefs. He would draw persuasive and creative conclusions based on the simple task at hand, reminding him what he knew and what he did not know. As obvious as that might imply, my experience has shown me that many people have blurred vision with what they think they know.

The known and unknown became clear to me, thanks to the aforementioned education I had from Solon High School and my own appetite for learning. If my learning involved a job description or policy position, I could recite it from memory. Understanding new market products and the manuals needed in an operations environment to deliver said products and services meant having a mind for detail.

I remember a manager by the name of Randy, a truly nice guy, telling me, "John, having a good memory is half the battle with problem-solving." More than a decade later, when taking seminars with a global, faith-based career development company, who casually suggested a job opening in Los Angeles, California (which I wasn't about to take serious, given the starting salary and cost of living adjustment), the executive director and founder told me my retention skills were extraordinary. I had banking to thank for that skill. You cannot excel in production and operations management without a good memory. Working in operations meant knowing routing symbols for scores of affiliated banks, account number/branch assignments, numerous line item accounting fields, not to mention multiple batch processing methods. Reconciliation and settlement had daily, monthly, quarterly and yearly applications.

Management by Objective was a huge initiative in our business. It never stopped. And numbers told stories. Numbers, goals and stories pretty much define a budget. Working with numbers, solving problems, learning systems, being mentored on personnel evaluations and cooperative work relationships, together with learning production management meant constant change and critical mass. One thing was always leading to another. All of which was about serving our customers and stockholders well and doing so within budget guidelines. Between banking classes, numerous seminars and workshops, I was becoming a specialist in my field. A decade and a couple promotions later it would make me and others commodities in our field. The world of work evolved into the age of specialization and division of labor.

Slowly, but surely, I was making gains in my career, but not without needed patience and tolerance. I had a quick tongue and was out-spoken with superiors that were showing their incompetence, power-mongering and need for self-importance. It was a flattering time in my career, creating a dependence on myself (as a "go to" guy). My willingness to learn and work was unmistaken. Wanting to (the very essence of motivation) learn, was, without doubt, due to my childhood habits with reading and wanting to make others look good (not just myself).

Having knowledge – whether it related to conflict resolution, juggling multiple tasks and details or being creative on the job – was like having a weapon. Words have always mattered to me. I would take painstaking effort to choose the right word(s) for the right situation, whether writing a report or completing an evaluation. And that got me a reputation, both good and bad. For some colleagues, it would mean feeling threatened or my usurping their authority. Too many times during my career I've encountered superiors that were more ego-involved than success-oriented. By osmosis I'd learn what kind of manager I did NOT want to become (just as I felt about what kind of father I did not want to become).

Let me give you an example. Banks, like many large corporations, are fond of their policy-driven form letters. There were many times in customer service when the bank might have to apologize for an oversight or error caused by an overpaid stop payment order, misfiled check or posting error for a check or deposit. At times, I preferred to personalize the letters, making them look less like a form letter and more like a letter of sincere apology. The changes would be subtle. On stop payment problems, especially, I felt it was important for the bank to acknowledge a customer's intent (purpose for the negotiable transaction, such as: payment for a brake repair on a car or dissatisfaction with a household repair). The "story" aspect, if you will. Customers generally appreciated being understood. I would look for subordinate points of agreement when negotiating a settlement between the warring factions (maker of check vs. payee). By diffusing emotions and absorbing their anger, I would usually be able to get all parties on the same page. Most the time they would agree to a solution, without the bank taking a total loss. I got great satisfaction out of solving their problem! And my correspondence reflected it. So did our write-offs! Such a tactic also empowers the customer, letting them have some control over the outcome.

One of my managers did not like my letter-writing form and style. He would rip my letters apart (sometimes literally, just for effect, or drama as we say today). He would criticize them, seemingly enjoying the criticism just a bit too much. So, one day I took one of his form letters from the file and changed only the recipient name and details (amount, payee, etc.). You guessed it: He ripped it to shreds! It told me what I wanted to know: That his "constructive criticism" had nothing to do with teaching me form. It was all about his ego.

I filed away that lesson from the University of Life, knowing one day I would do things differently. I was fascinated with Walt Disney's management style. I knew my own style was different than those I worked for, not with. Some of my immediate superiors relished asserting their authority, while flashing their titles with constant reminders of their "entitlement." While I was limited as that time with how much I could exercise my own managing philosophies, I was more a draw leader (vs. "The driver" type). Draw leadership is akin to shared leadership (Disney's culture) and participative management. A few years later, after achieving the goal of becoming a bank officer, my philosophical differences would put me on a collision course with the new executive boss (a non-banker...hired gun brought in from the outside, outside meaning out-of-town). Banking was changing. So was I.

One of my primary responsibilities as a bank supervisor was that of employee evaluations. Companion to that function was the updating of operating manuals and job procedures. For the rest of my career, I would be amused by how people perceived their role vs. that which was clearly spelled out in a job description. The breakdown was not always the employee. Often the true cause to poor communications and employee relations was the failure of management to keep job descriptions current, then communicate those expectations to their employees. Having been an entry-level employee accelerating into a first-level supervisory role, I identified with both line employees and management.

Thus, communications became a primary thrust in my own development. Whether conflict was between fellow employees or with customers, it seemed to me most people listened to reply, not understand. Too often my interpersonal experiences gave me reason to believe people were more interested in who was right or wrong, rather than *what* was right or wrong. Often I would find myself composing a well-constructed memorandum to superiors (remember, operations is a detail world, whereby the devil is, indeed, in the details), explaining a problem or solution, only to have it summarily dismissed. Later, when I had more authority, I would change our work culture by acting like a host during meetings. Often I would remind someone, when making a presentation that it is okay for others to critique it. I'd say, "There's always something wrong with any good idea." Synergy is good. Likewise, when someone has a bad idea, it doesn't mean there might not be a kernel of truth to some aspect that helps move the ball forward.

Anyway, my earlier encounters with management evidenced too many that wanted to assert their titles. Yelling or getting loud was the response to challenging their so-called authority. It actually did surprise me how often superiors would show their insecurity or lack of self-confidence by defaulting to yelling or temper tantrums. That kind of work environment led to many turf battles, CYA tactics and posturing between colleagues. It was like having one camp vs. another camp in the workplace. Intellectual discourse and healthy debate was undermined by ignorance and verbal putdowns (one-upmanship and gotcha moments). It was a sign of the times. While always respecting someone's position (title), my respect for the people that once kept me in awe waned.

Too many imposters in the workplace for my intuitive taste. It made me angry, but I tried to control it. More dynamically, the country was angry too. President Nixon had lied to Americans, resulting in his shame and resignation. His replacement by succession became Gerald Ford, who would go on to hit people with stray golf shots. Following Ford, Jimmy Carter would micro-manage an economic downturn, as well as misdirect an ill-fated rescue mission in the Middle East. Meanwhile, Cleveland's race relations were strained. The mayor accidently set his hair on fire, making our great city the butt of late night talk show hosts. Even our beloved Cuyahoga River caught on fire (oil slick). Worse, the mayor's wife turned down an invitation to the White House because it was her "bowling night."

It was a goofy time in Ohio's Northeastern parts. Something happened to our once proud city on the lake. Everyone was calling it "the mistake on the lake." Years later, when out of state for business or pleasure, I almost did not want to tell people where I was from.

Something Happened, ironically was also the name of Joseph Heller's 1974 novel, quite popular at the time. The author had established his reputation through his first best-selling book, *Catch – 22*. I was in the business world at that time, adjusting to a new self-image and my role in society.

The author's narrative through the main character paralleled my own experience at work: While promotions were coming my way and with others, the sanity of the workplace – if not the country – seemed in question! Contrary to what a high school teacher wrote in my yearbook, I was not seeing "hard work being rewarded by success." Like the main character in the book, leaders around me were becoming hypocritical and, excuse me – but quite immoral in some of their personal conduct (sometimes on the job). Welcome to the real world John. I don't judge people, but making valued judgments of right and wrong – choices, if you will, has a place in our conduct.

It was more than reckless assumptions; it was clear to me that loyalty was a diminishing characteristic in the workplace. Truth seemed negotiable. Sad to say, but truth, loyalty and integrity were no longer valued on the job. In my idealistic youth, that hurt! The new buzz word in the workplace became "survival."

Survival was something I knew about.

Merriam – Webster Dictionary would have us understand that survival is a "state of continuing to live or exist in spite of difficult conditions." The gentleman that brought me into banking had connections, both through his wife (social worker) and the community. Some of these contacts had impressive credentials, including affiliation with large hospitals and area sports teams. All quite humbling for a guy that would have easily won "Most Likely Not To Succeed" in high school. "Reject" still stuck in my mind too. At the behest of my influential banking mentors, suddenly I had so-called experts informing me as to the full nature of my cancerous arm. Hearing a prestigious physician for a National Football League team explain osteogenic sarcoma shocked me, making me contemplate my life expectancy – again, but this time with clinical, hard data – not based on muscle weakness, bone ache, nerve pain and fatigue.

Thankfully, my life was busy! I had no time to buy trouble or be negative. Vocationally, I had an increasing workload and much to learn about my trade. Personally, my friends kept me busy with golf dates and numerous occasions for dinner. There were college campuses to visit, since many of my friends lived in dormitories. My nature was to "entertain and inform," so I devoted time to making my friends laugh. At work, I wanted to make my bosses look good! I expected them to reciprocate.

I was sadly and often disappointed. Many…too many….were "in it" for themselves. It was the growing nature of a new generation – the Me Generation.

Unexpectedly, I had a sense of déjà vu. I felt like I didn't belong…I did not fit in.

Just as I was riding a wave of new learning, making new friends and excelling in the workplace, I was being told that the survival rate for my childhood cancer was 2% (with mortality seldom over the age of forty). My foster mother, it seemed to me, was in and out of the hospital with her own cancer battles all her adult life. It was depressing. She leaned on me a lot. Most the time she would confide in me, telling me "Dad doesn't care!"…"He can't handle things"…and so on. Her face, especially her lips and nose, had become horribly disfigured from surgical procedures. She was terribly self-conscious.

My foster father would remind me often that I should have remained at the home in Solon, that mother needed my care and comfort. One day he would be bragging to others about my being a successful businessman – a banker! It made *him* look good. Another day, when I hoped he might say something…anything that would suggest he might give me a little credit, some small measure of praise just would not be forthcoming. When visiting, inevitably something would trigger his anger. Still, I kept trying to win his acceptance. The guy was a mystery to me. I never gave up on him or the possibility that one day he might bring himself to say he loved me. I visited one evening after work, only to be directed to the bedroom where I would find my cancer-ridden foster mother laying in her own feces, soiled and in a fetal position. The old man simply told me to "clean the mess up."

The scenario described above occurred more than once. It was depressing to see them. Yet, I felt a need to "be there" for my foster mom. On each successive occasion she would tell me of her impending death…wish. Despite the death wishes, she would rebound…for a while…until the next time. Each episode of her cancer bouts left her spirit in decline. It played on my mind as I contemplated my own fate.

I would return to my work, only to hear a new boss berate his staff. Many years later that executive, through a mutual contact at another job, would apologize to me over the telephone for his earlier bout with alcoholism. He told me how hard he was on people, including his own family. Frankly, I respected him for manning up to his behavior. Unfortunately, that's not how I felt when working under his tyranny. When working with him he literally SCREAMED at inanimate objects and people. Had I not associated his behavior with my foster father or the fact that his rants were unbecoming of a professional executive, I would have laughed. It was almost comical.

Whatever it was, it was not fun to go to work. I worked faithfully and hard anyway. Fair to say, my attitude – when giving the boss the benefit of the doubt – was extended to my foster father (or perhaps the other way around). With all my foster father's faults, his work ethic and trade skills were impressive and impacting on me. The lessons learned from simply just respecting his skills (a subordinate point of agreement) would never be lost on me. Thus, I would learn to always look for the best in others, no matter what their faults might be.

A Victory March

Though I had accepted Christ into my life, the Lord seemed distant to me. So did grace. A "happy face" would be seen by my friends (especially my surrogate families). It was all an act. Masking my true feelings could have earned me an Academy Award. Books were still my friends.

Years later, 2007, to be exact, while renting a home, we would experience what the media would come to call "The One Hundred Year Flood." Many Midwestern states, Ohio included, were swamped by severe storms and flooding. Hundreds upon hundreds of homes went without electricity for several days, causing millions of dollars in property damage. We had nearly four feet of raw sewage backed up in our basement. My *friends* (books) were destroyed! Many of our wedding gifts were ruined too. "Warehouse" was the euphemism I gave to our basement, where many of our personal belongings were in storage. One book, among a few bookshelves of other surviving books, was *The Gospel According To Peanuts*, written by Robert Short, who, of course, was indebted to legendary Peanuts creator Charles Schultz. Their unusual theological humor, sure enough, became a form of saving grace. Humor always has been the best medicine!

Peanuts had become a source of humor for many while I was growing up. The popular expression by its characters, saying "Good grief" was a contradiction, so one would think. *The Gospel According to Peanuts,* however, explained in moments of adversity that two kinds of grief existed. There was the not so good grief cleverly described by the author, using 2nd Corinthians 7:10 as his lesson: "For godly grief produces a repentance that leads to salvation and brings no regret, but worldly grief produces death." Short goes on to explain that Christians celebrate "Good Friday," though it was the day Christ was crucified. Therefore, like Christ, suffering can be interpreted as a passage. Hence, "Good Grief!" Thank God that book survived!

Having planted the importance of that book and many others, I return to my days at the bank. Between my foster father's continued criticisms and demands, together with the changing management scene at work, one wrought with paranoia, turf battles and outbursts unbecoming of a leader, I was discouraged. My spirit was greatly challenged, at work and with my foster parents. But – it was not broken! Like the mighty Cleveland Browns defense, still known as a powerhouse in those days, I would bend, but not break!

Thank God for those books!

WORLD OF WORK MORPHS INTO PERSONAL ENRICHMENT & VOCATIONAL ENLIGHTENMENT

It was 1970. *Let It Be* could easily be recognized as a song by the Beatles. Just as easily some could stretch their imagination. Its meaning euphemistically could be "Amen." The song and the Beatles were embroiled in controversy. So was I. The forces of change were well under way at work, as merger mania took the country by storm. Thus, work had become more challenging, yet strangely rewarding. While the acrimonious Beatles and I were seeking words of wisdom vocationally and personally it was not to be.

I was looking for answers to all the chaos in life at work and home. Answers were not enough. It took a couple decades later, but by the grace of God, perspective on my search for answers was given in the lyrics of Scott Wesley Brown and Greg Nelson's song called *When Answers Are Not Enough*. Its lyrics open with "you have faced the mountains of desperation, you have climbed, you have fought, [and] you have won. But this valley that lies coldly before you casts a shadow you cannot overcome." The artists go on with their lyrics and music, guiding the lost and searching towards deeper understanding. Instead of asking why something happened, we focus instead on what is the experience teaching us? Where is it leading us? Eventually, we can live our lives triumphantly – through the tears. When answers are not enough, there is Jesus! When answers are not enough, He is there. But such wisdom was not immediately forthcoming when I was twenty-one.

So, for too many years I had stumbled, falling forwards. Metaphoric mountains to climb always seemed to be in my pathway.

I would climb them with steadfast determination, despite the shadows stalking me along the way. I disguised them well with my sunny disposition. How right author Lloyd Ogilvie was when writing in his book, *Making Stress Work for You,* when describing our tendencies to "repress the stress we don't express."

Unfortunately, that friendly book would not find my library shelf until the mid-1980's.

The Lord was in my life. So were my families of another name. Work and school kept me occupied. I was able to make a decent living, take some well-earned vacations and improve on my education. Yet, creative as my life was becoming, peace of mind was far off. I was a work in progress, by the grace of God.

Looking back now, I believe this time period was the genesis of the title of my first book, *Your Pathway to Personal Enrichment & Vocational Enlightenment.* Later chapters will canvas my journey of the current millennium, where I will elaborate on the mutually exclusive nature of personal enrichment and vocational enlightenment. But, suffice to say, it was four decades earlier when experience was seeding, only to be harvested in the autumn of my years. A book hound was I, but never did I dream of writing one (or two books). I have had many titles during my personal and professional life: Supervisor, manager, bank executive, board member, elder, chairman, speaker, entrepreneur and writer. None satisfy more than being a husband and father! In 1970 becoming a husband and father was just a dream. It was families of another name that made me dream the role of a family man.

FAMILIES OF ANOTHER NAME

Being estranged from my immediate family – my foster parents – was not of my choosing. I chose to love them anyway, even when hearing my foster mom tell me after another violent argument between she and her husband that "we shouldn't have gotten you; it was a mistake."

Even when concealing the painful memories of a tyrant who smacked me down when I couldn't get up, (the kitchen floor episode, when soothing my cancerous right arm against the heat register). I felt sorry for them, especially my foster mom.

At least, she tried...tried to feel love...to connect. As my foster mother became more emotionally dependent on me, given the absence of her husband's affections, we would play endless games of 500 Rummy. Anyone familiar with this card game knows of meld cards which extend a hand already shown on the table. Sometimes when discarding, a player will overlook the opportunity, allowing the opposing player to yell RUMMY, thus capturing the points as well. My foster mom loved catching me when I'd be careless on such a discard. It's memorable because it is one of the few things we did together that we both enjoyed. Plus, she would smile - despite the disfigured lip and nose - scarring from her numerous cancer surgeries...despite the emotional scars of being a battered wife. It was worth losing those points to see her beautiful smile.

In truth, everyday living in the Klein household was a day I sought their acceptance and love. Time and time again the expectation was not realized. At least, not with my foster dad. In the chapters to follow, I will share a death bed scene with my foster mother. In her case, as said – at least, she tried.

A Victory March

Friends & Friendship, a book written by Jerry and Mary White spoke to my heart. It reinforced my own notions on friends and family. There are friends and there are friends. And there is family. Their book helped me better understand the emotional depths of my own being toward those in my life that became friends…that became like family. It was a religious publication, making the life of Jesus Christ the foundation to all friendships, which they described as built upon the passages of time and effort, furthered by the essence of love, the trust of sharing, the example of sacrificing, the art of encouragement, shared spiritual moments, loyalty and fun. Truly, I was blessed with good friends by the grace of God. Other than bound books made of paper and glue being my friends, my flesh and blood friends became my family. Dr. Seuss wrote, "Be who you are and say what you feel because those who mind don't matter and those who matter don't mind."

My foster father would have no tolerance for self-expression. Children were to be seen, not heard, as the old saying goes. Speaking my mind could literally get me slapped across the face. I've often felt that my tendency to get chatty in casual conversations lends itself to those beginnings (overcompensating).

Regardless, fate had it that I would meet three families, who didn't mind what I had to say and share. Quite the contrary, they seemed interested in my opinions and encouraged me to open up. Interestingly, the three families I am going to share with you on these pages became close to me in my adult life. They were my saving grace because I was learning that being married to my job got old. I would come home (whether it be the unwelcoming environment of my foster parent's home or that of my lonely apartment), wondering is there life after work?

Three families made it possible for me to have my own family. Call them surrogates, substitutes or adopted families. Point is: They accepted me like family. And so it was: Each of them, uniquely my family.

The Leslie Family

Earlier in this book I mentioned this family when writing of the slow motion football games, the angel hair spaghetti and the tragic automobile accident. Unlike the other two families, the Leslie's were a part of my childhood. An uncle was the gentleman who recruited me into the banking profession. Tim Leslie and I would visit his Uncle Jim and Aunt Jean many times. I always enjoyed meeting his uncle because he was cool for an older guy. He had wit. And he had a scooter. I have become that man. Tim had a brother named Neil. Neil was extremely bright and precocious for his age. For a brief time we commuted together, taking an Erie Lackawanna train to school and work. We would arrive at Cleveland's downtown terminal, literally hanging on to handle bars positioned above the train steps. He would proceed to St. Ignatius High School, where quite possibly he was teaching the teachers. He was that smart. Still is. To this day, we remain very close. When I would seek safe haven at the Leslie home, it was Neil that made me feel most welcomed and comfortable. Intellectually, our humor was in another realm than the rest of the planet.

Having a conversation with Neil is like having a playground with word play and off-beat humor for a joy ride. To this day, he will call me from an airport, taking me on a conversational journey unlike anyone else I know – but for the exception of my writing buddy Colin. Neil knows of my penchant for the word grace. Practically every time we talk over the telephone he will steer the conversation to Grace, using the word as a proper noun.

"So John, how is Grace?" He'll ask. It never stops. Neil and everyone in the Leslie Family simply made me feel at home, whether it was in their home on Aurora Road or their cottage south of Cleveland. It was a safe place where I didn't have to listen to screaming or worrying if I was going to get slapped and thumped around. The Leslie Family was the first place that made me not feel threatened or self-conscious. Their home was an alternative to the chaos a thousand feet away. As said, it was safe haven.

The Hach Family

When my classmate Tom introduced me to Dave Hach in the late 1960's, asking me to join him and Dave for a golfing vacation in Myrtle Beach, South Carolina, neither of us knew then how great an impact Dave and I would have, not just with one another, but with our respective families that would follow. Another individual on that memorable trip had a strong liking for really cheap motels. He also liked to complain about health ailments that got a bit too personal. As it goes in group dynamics, Dave and I immediately gravitated to one another for the sake of escaping this guy's constant bellyaching and deep-seeded desire to sleep with cockroaches.

Being young and stupid, our humor was ruthless, making light of the older guy with strange personal taste and habits. We made excuses to travel in the same car coming home, refusing to eat or sleep where others dared (though we were not given a choice one night). We hit it off immediately, him liking the music of Johnny Mathis…Me, Sinatra. Dave worked at a local A & P grocery store. His work ethic and commuting to college coincided with my work philosophies and downtown commute. We enjoyed dining out. We both loved spaghetti and steak! Most importantly, we had a passion for golf. We shared a belief in chivalry, meaning we sought companionship with a lady. We had class. Old-fashioned romantics were we, but such was our taste for woman, wine and life itself.

When returning from the golf vacation, our friendship grew quickly, resulting in golf or dinner weekly. We enjoyed each other's company. We were, in fact, good company. The manner in which we treated the other, I believe, was impressionable on the choices we each made for that special lady in our lives. The value of good company became even more meaningful later in life when relocation, death and coaching would introduce me to new frontiers and new relationships. Anyway, Dave had invited me into their home where I met his mother. Today we might call it a man-date. Meeting Mrs. Hach was love at first sight. The woman – like Mrs. Leslie – was a saint! Her countenance and composure was unlike any woman I had ever met in my life. She was a working mother. Quite possibly, she may have been one of the most efficient women on the planet! Dolores Hach would give this Mother Theresa smile, making your problems go away immediately. She could whip up a four-course meal in fifteen minutes. She had the sweetest face, owl-like (she actually did have an owl collection of miniature figurines). Mrs. Hach was very intelligent. She was an executive secretary, with the emphasis on executive.

Mrs. Hach knew about my foster mother and father. Like the Leslie Family, they attended the same church. Mrs. Hach, having considerable insight about my foster father, never pressed me or embarrassed me over details of my upbringing. She just knew. What she knew best was how to love her family and her family's friends. She made me feel at home in a way that made me feel like Dave's brother. In fact, as the years went by, Dave and I acted like we were brothers. And that is why this segment deserves so much space. What was to follow was something out of a Hallmark made-for-television movie.

After work at the bank the Hach household was the place to be a few times a week (including weekends). Friday nights were devoted to dressing up for dinner. We would don suit and ties for either the Brown Derby Restaurant or a little tavern on Aurora Road that featured all-you-can-eat spaghetti. By then I was referred to as "son #4." Mr. and Mrs. Hach were as loving a couple as the Leslie's. They actually enjoyed being in the company of one another, always laughing about something. I became a regular staple at their house for dinner, leading to many jokes about ketchup. Okay – so I like ketchup on my steak! Mr. Hach was fondly called "Iron." Ed Hach was a cop when I met him. Later he would have a few other jobs too, but he was best known for being a retired policeman…one whose badge got "rusty" – hence "Iron" being dubbed as his nickname. He truly was one of the funniest men I've ever met in my life. Hands down!

Mr. Ed "Iron" Hach had gained a few pounds later in life, but his head was handsome. If sculpted, the artist would need to reference Bob Hope's ski-slope nose, Steve McQueen's hair and comedian/artist Red Skelton's smile. He was a dapper fellow. As I wrote in a tribute given after his death, "…his most prized possessions were not the new Cadillac he craved, the trains he kept for a hobby, nor his jewelry; and, it certainly was not his golf clubs or toolbox (unused, which he would be the first to laugh at). No – his most prized possessions were his family. For almost four decades he would include me in their family. More importantly, the Hach Family included my wife and two sons, as if they were their own grandchildren. We celebrated every Christmas together! I described Mr. Hach as one with "Emeritus in Abstract Philosophy and Humor."

His Ironisms would rival the nomenclature of Yogi Berra. His best was "if you have no alternative, you have no problem." Think about that. The guy was no ordinary man. He was funny and he was smart like a fox. I learned a lot from him.

One anecdote that stands out was the night I dropped by the Hach household after a depressing evening with my dying foster father at the hospital. I had taken a limited in-hospital caregiving role for a man who never expressed or showed any love towards me. I was trying to ease his pain by working with the doctors, which meant making some decisions about what kind of comfort care would be afforded him in his last days. He would hear nothing of the kind.

He would moan loudly about not wanting to hear anything negative. "I only want POSITIVE stuff," he would scream, while directing expletives at me! When telling Iron this, the master comedian –

philosopher says to me, "John, this is what you do. You go back to the hospital and tell your father, 'Dad, you are POSITIVELY going to die in two or three weeks!'" I confess. I laughed.

Of course, it is dark humor. God forgive me, but I needed it. This is why. My foster father's last words – just after spitting in my face and raising his arm to hit me – were "YOU ARE NOT MY BLOOD!" Under my breath, I whispered "Thank God." I intercepted his weakened and emaciated arm. It was the first time in my life I was able to stop him. He was a broken man, humiliated by my small defensive gesture. On the other hand, Ed Hach was everything Tom Klein was not. When kissing Mr. Hach on the head before his passing, there was no doubt he heard my words, telling him thanks for showing me how to be a loving husband and father. The man taught me how to laugh – often! Chances are when entering the gates of Heaven, he had angels laughing. Mr. Ed "Iron" Hach was more like a father than any other man in my life. He had an unabashed joy for life. As I matured into a family man my own philosophy and humor greatly matched his example. Simply put, I love life (even when it is tough)!

Dave Hach and I became life-long friends. For a short time our wives worked together. He and his wife, Bev, had two daughters, whom for all intents and purposes were like cousins to the two boys my wife and I would raise. Later in life, not long ago, as my wife was dying from cancer, so was my friend Dave. Dave died in February 2010. He was so ill that I represented my honorary brother at his father's funeral. While still living in Ohio and before Dave's passing, I met him at a Cracker Barrel Restaurant parking lot, nearby a hotel he stayed at while returning from a cancer treatment. He handed me an old May Company Department Store box, measuring 4 ¼" by 11" by 2" deep.

The treasured box contained a gag gift given when we were still teenagers. The Hach Family had bought me new Jack Nicklaus golf clubs. No one had ever given me a gift like that before in my life. The May Company box contained head covers for the new woods. They were really lame "Golf Mate Dial-A-Mitt" covers. You could take a tee and literally dial the numbered wood of choice. It is something a clown might use. It was a gift to make us all laugh. And we laughed for more than three decades, having exchanged that silly gift, back and forth, and every year thereafter. We'd build suspense every year, no matter whose turn it was to present the annual gift. It became the highlight of every Christmas gift exchange.

When Dave handed me the box at the parking lot, long before Christmas – I knew what it meant. I am holding it now as I type this page. The symbolism will never be lost on me.

The McGilvray Family

In 1969 America was saying good riddance to a decade of assassinations. We had lost John F. and Robert F. Kennedy, as well as Martin Luther King. Our country was embroiled in a terrible war. Some things don't change. A new decade awaited, but it was 1969 that would pave the way with the likes of Woodstock, a farm in New York hosting in excess of 350,000 fans listening to anti-war lyrics. Butch Cassidy and the Sundance Kid were running from the law, just as many young draft-dodgers were doing the same.

Music was all over the charts. Barry McGuire was singing about the *Eve of Destruction*. Bob Dylan was *Blowing in the Wind*. Johnny Cash reminded us that *Daddy Sang Bass* and Zager and Evans optimistically, yet fatalistically were singing *In the Year 2525* (if man were still alive). It was a strange time. Thankfully, for my generation, 1969 also gave birth to one of the professional football's greatest athletes, Brett Favre – who loved playing in cold weather. Without him, Cheese-heads would never have found their way into the Urban Dictionary. Most significantly, 1969 was the deadline year that John F. Kennedy challenged America to place a man on the moon. We did when an Ohioan astronaut, Neil Armstrong, stepped onto the surface of the moon.

1969 was also the year that Donald McGilvray stepped into my life. Don and I worked together at Society National Bank in Cleveland, Ohio. Unlike Neil Armstrong, our feet remained on earth. After work, Don liked playing football in the worst of Ohio's winter weather. We called it the Ice Bowl. Whenever his residential street would freeze over, I could count on spending the night at Don's home as a guest. I was also trying hard to play a game that was hard for me – given the limitations of my right arm. I would protect the arm, while trying my best to hide my intentions from anyone noticing. It was hard to do when playing cut-throat neighborhood games in the streets of Cleveland.

Don and I became friends, frequently sharing lunch time together in or out of the bank. Often we would play cards (Rummy) and discuss social issues and politics. Being the book hound that I was, his family reminded me of the famous American families, like the Kennedy's (though their politics were far from the McGilvray's). Nevertheless, the Kennedy's were known for dinnertime discussions, especially on the plight of the poor or the state of the nation. Every time I had dinner or breakfast with the McGilvray's they would enlist a healthy debate on current events, whether it be the war, Nixon's trade policies or the economy.

Don's father, Clifton Ellis McGilvray was a community branch banking manager for forty-one years. He was a family man. And he liked golf. He understood and practiced the old axiom "know your customer." We could use his kind today in this world of service providers. He was a gentle and kind man. He was also prone to enjoy a good prank. Don lived at home, during the time we worked together. Often I would be invited to spend the night. When Don's brother moved out, I inherited his bedroom.

The McGilvray family was hospitable. Mrs. McGilvray and her husband were curious about me, always making me feel welcome in their home. While that was nice, I fretted that my friend Don would get sick of seeing me. But I had to admit, I enjoyed their company.

As our friendship endured, Don would learn more about my past and the circumstances behind my arm. When learning more about both, his manner towards me became more compassionate. When competing, he would be mellower in temperament. We would still be fierce competitors, but there was no doubt in the change of attitude. Like Dave, he became like a brother.

While my faith is strong, I don't often give testimonials (though, this book, obviously is exactly that: a testimonial). As I have grown older, foaming at the mouth about my faith has simply not been my style. So, it surprised me some years ago when Don would acknowledge my lifestyle and behavior as an influence for his own Christian commitment. It is incredibly humbling to have another human being express that kind of gratitude. He gives me too much credit, but hearing such would make any among us beam with healthy pride. I don't let it go to my head because, as we know, pride can be such a foolish thing. To this day his faith is unshakable. He loves the Lord, as do I. And I love him for it – like a brother.

Don eventually left banking to go into another field (which was a great call). He prospered well by obeying his calling. Before leaving, however, we shared a ride to work one day when suddenly we saw two Great Danes – excuse me – copulating on a West 25th street sidewalk.

Don nearly drove his 1968 Camaro – with the Beach Boys wailing *Good Vibrations* on his 8-track player – into a street post! We laughed so hard we nearly wrecked. It was just an adolescent-like thing, the two of us uncontrollably guffawing.

From that moment on The Order of the Danes was conceived. To this day I am referred to as the senior member of the Order, dubbed Top (Sr.) Dawg. As tradition would have it, the Order remains, passing on to a new generation, including and ordaining Don's son, Clif – my honorary nephew (named after his wonderful grandfather, Clifton). Like the golf head covers that Dave Hach and I annually exchanged for more than three decades, Don and I would swap "barks" and "high signs" (like a dog holding its paws up, begging). When speaking on the phone, we will invariably acknowledge one another with barks, beginning and ending every call.

Same with my buddy, Drew. We just couldn't grow up. I figure if comedians Carol Burnett and Tim Conway can still act silly, later into their years, so can we.

Don and I would spend countless evenings playing basketball, football, and golf or watching old black and white re-runs of *Combat*, starring Vic Morrow. During the 1960's it was considered the most realistic portrayal of World War II. When not at his house, he would hang at my apartment where he would claim my infamous pumpkin-colored orange couch as his bed.

Two pound frozen On-Cor TV dinners became a main entrée for dinner each and every occasion. For years it would be a standing inside joke between us. Four decades later we remain very close. What I remember from our early years is how we could discuss most anything on the social or political landscape without ever losing our senses of humor. We could be serious, yet stay on the lighter side of life. I also remember how we never missed a beat on corresponding with one another when he served his country in Germany. It seemed like we would both be writing letters weekly.

Lesson learned? Example matters. Without saying anything, how I lived my life spoke volumes to a brother in need. My friend gave his life to Christ, not because of anything I said, but how I lived my life – imperfect as it was. It was a lesson in humility. As always, when holding that torch to light another person's path, it only brightens our own.

In the Book of Matthew it is written (Chapter 7:16), "you can identify them by their fruit, that is, by the way they act." The McGilvray

Family, beginning with Ruth and Clifton, were such an example – first to their sons, including Don and his family…and to me. They taught me how a real family solves differences gracefully. They gave me a brother in Christ, one that allowed me to have the incredible distinction of being an honorary uncle to my friend Don and Wally's (Don's wife) son and two daughters. I am blessed.

AUTHOR'S INTERLUDE

By now dear reader you have a fair idea of the early childhood struggles I endured, like so many others. Fortuitously, opportunities for personal and professional growth were developing, mostly because of good people that kept coming into my life when I felt most challenged. I maintain that this was not happenstance or dumb luck. It was God's Grace! But grace was not always self-evident when going through early trials and tribulations.

It was as if God had provided me an umbrella to shield me wherever I went…whatever my toils. Later in life, grace was revealed to me though quiet times of reflection and consolidation.

Earlier chapters narrate health issues and brokenness in a seemingly successful suburban family home. At the same time, the work culture was changing. Self-interest and greed were replacing social conscience and business benevolence. Times were a changing (just as Dylan said they were). Though I had declared my independence by going it alone, personal matters were growing in intensity and uncertainty. Surrogate parents were calling me one of their own, making "families of another name" my families. Without those families…those friends, there would have been no harmony between my personal and vocational life. Having said that, at times bouncing between various friends and their families made me feel as if I were a vagabond…or in some kind of real-life pinball game.

Life with my foster father had progressed, somewhat. He had mellowed – so it seemed. He would brag about my relative success in the banking world because it made *him* look good. When seeing him, he still couldn't bring himself to ever say anything kind to me. He was approaching retirement and sought the same passion as mine – golf! And, oh how he wanted to compete with me. Ostensibly, he would welcome me more often to his home. He, relaxing his verbal and physical weapons for a short spell, reminded me of what nations do when conflicted: détente. Naively, I saw this apparent change of heart as a gesture for outreach…a matter of reconciliation. How wrong I was!

Meantime, the senior banker's wife and social worker, mentioned earlier, thought it would be a good idea that I meet my biological father. An arrangement was made for me to meet him at his residence, basically a flophouse. It went horribly wrong. He was terribly inebriated when we met. Yet, he was conscious of who I was, calling me the "son that came home to take care of him." He was delusional. I was conflicted. Though I had some practice with my foster father, at that moment, I felt helpless with what to do about my biological father's total lack of sobriety. I was on an emotional roller-coaster. He grew angry at me when I told him I had better leave. He actually swung at me! Meek as I was, I gently guided him to a chair, sitting him….kissing him on the forehead and softly telling him "I have to go." I never saw him again. Driving home that night, stunned, all I could think of was how I now had two fathers who enjoyed swinging their fists at me!

All the surrogate parents and families of another name did not change the stark reality of my home existence: that of feeling unloved. Though more independent and occupied by work, the sense of not belonging or fitting in festered my private thoughts. I was insecure – still. The social model we traditionally call the nuclear family – one that loves unconditionally – was unknown to me.

Staying at a safe distance, yet trying to still get along with my foster father became mission impossible. Time and time again, public encounters with him – whether it be in restaurants or on golf courses – became an embarrassment. Brewing ahead would be several episodes of violence – none of which I was prepared for or saw coming. Most memorable was a visit at the farm house my foster parents owned in Western Pennsylvania. My neighbor with two boys joined me and my two boys for an overnight camping trip, to cut wood for our fire-burning stoves.

After a night of camp fires, stories and good fun with the kids, I went to the main house, to retrieve some items for breakfast. My foster father confronted me in the kitchen with a threatening look on his face. He held up two documents. They were insurance waiver forms – for beneficiaries. Before dying, my foster mother had worked a factory job for several years, having told me her intentions to open two insurance policies for her two grandsons (with the expressed purpose for their education).

My foster father roughly grabbed my right arm, holding me tight and twisting my arm! With fire in his eyes he told me to sign the waiver forms or he would break my "bad arm!" He meant it! Without thought, I did so. I didn't give a damn about the money – whether it was from my foster mother or him claiming rights to it. I regret that decision. My neighbor walked in the house, startled with disbelief, confusion and, perhaps, shock. I never spoke to him at length about the cause of the altercation. It was too personal and embarrassing. I know this: It was not my foster father's money! My mother worked hard for that money.

Even in her death, he abused her. The old man denied what was rightly meant for both my sons' educations. "Hurt me," I thought; "but, don't hurt your own grandchildren!" Having been on the receiving end of his vicious blows, I had every reason to believe he would have followed through on his threat to break my re-sectioned arm. Still – I repeat – If given the opportunity for a retake, I would not have conceded to his demands.

A few years later my brother-in-law accompanied me to the home in Solon, where he, too, witnessed an episode where my foster father came at me, threatening to put me through a large wall mirror. At the time I immediately remembered a similar incident, when as a child I ran from my foster father – only to run through a glass door. The scar, thank God, was linear on my wrist, not across the wrist. My foster mom called the police chief – a personal friend of my parents. He came to our home and she had me treated. No record was officially recorded. My brother-in-law, immediately recognizing that my foster father was out of control, directed me through the same door, except this time I walked through it. He commented on the insanity of the moment and the rage of the man – totally unprovoked. It was just best to leave what happened behind and move on. And we did.

No doubt readers might wonder if any of my story regarding the violent and abusive nature of my foster father could actually happen in real life. If anything, I have toned it down. In fact, for years I suppressed and understated most my emotions with respect to my foster home. The adopted brother had some exposure to this violence, but suffered few first-hand encounters such as I did.

****

As you already know, eventually I met my wife and raised a family. It amazes me how quickly the years went by. Thankfully, the experiences Connie and I created replaced the sour memories from the foster home. I interrupted this story with an interlude because it adds perspective to the story. When taking college classes or engaged in a meeting, I'd find it annoying when instructors or superiors exercised "avoidance" tactics (vs. approach), by saying, "We'll cover that next week" or "Hold that thought until we cover that material." I just wanted to tell them "Answer the damn question!"

It is why I won't watch a presidential press conference anymore. By giving you a glimpse into my future, the only thing I avoid is this story being just another "from the cradle to the grave" book. Again, as Paul Harvey used to say, "Now the rest of the story!"

In the 1980's my perspective on life was changing. My foster parents were both still alive and still being difficult. What changed was my experience. Older and wiser, I could better manage the emotional involvement. Connie provided balance in my life. She would be supportive where and when I needed home to anchor the chaos at work or with my foster parents.

I repeat, personal enrichment & vocational enlightenment – by the Grace of God – were written on my heart long before my mind concocted the sub-title one night in the back of a cargo van. God was way ahead of me. But, abiding faith prevailed. And it was in the 1980's that I once again turned to my books for friendship.

A child psychologist, Jonathan Kellerman had emerged on the literary scene. His own origins are that of cancer survivorship. His early writings were devoted to the emotional and intellectual development of children with cancer. I appreciated how he would later write novels, showcasing an ability to work backwards, taking the reader on a journey with back stories of his cast of distinctive characters. It actually swayed me to develop some compassion for my foster father, wondering about his father and his early child-rearing. I suppose I even became a bit guilty with what is known as the "Stockholm Syndrome," a psychological phenomenon, whereby hostages show sympathy toward their captors. As I will reveal later in this book, I would pay a dear price for giving him the benefit of the doubt. In hindsight, the price was worth it – for the lessons learned.

It was only when meditating on the merits of writing this book that a close writing friend of mine sent me a link to the 1997 movie, *Good*

Will Hunting. Matt Damon and Robin Williams, respectfully, portray two men, Will Hunting and Sean Maguire. They have an intense and emotional scene when Sean tells the young protégé, "IT'S NOT YOUR FAULT!"

The older mentor repeats and repeats the admonition. The abuse may have been of another kind, but the impact was the same. It has only taken thirty-five plus years, but between Kellerman's novels, *Good Will Hunting* and my close friend Colin, I think I finally had come to terms with the enormous guilt I have hidden from my family and friends for all these years.

Often I would ponder a notion, one which is played out this way: Had my foster parents not kept me, I couldn't help but think that just maybe their lives would have been happier (especially with how they related to one another). It was my belief, that because of me, my biological foster brother and sister might have stayed in their home – making them happy and together. Also not lost in that notion was the possibility that Mike and Joe, my two other foster brothers, might have stayed in the Klein home. I felt for most of my life that my needs and health issues were the root cause of the growing chasm that grew between my foster mother and father.

While writing this book I've made peace with the foolishness of that repressed nonsense. But, it was books and my friends that gave this "Encourager" one of his own patented "gentle nudges"…in the right direction. Indeed, I can safely assume it was grace in action.

****

As you can see, as author, I am exercising some writer's discretion, literally and literarily, on form. While most autobiographers prefer the chronological approach (mentioned earlier) by mapping their life from birth, I am choosing to tell you my story by departing from such form in favor of anecdotes and narratives – as they build upon the theme of grace and how I became known as The Encourager. By doing so, it is my hope that other people I share in my story remind you of those in your own life that made you a better person…or challenged you to become a better person (…and yes, sometimes, even enemies motivate us to a higher calling).

My main purpose in telling my story is based on two words imbedded in the last paragraph: grace and encouragement. In the pop-culture, shock-oriented world we live in today, which is more critical than correct, it's my belief there is a profound lack of grace shown in both the workplace and at home. Too many among us act as if we are self-made successes. That is ridiculous. As country music star Tim McGraw sings, "We all take different paths in life, but no matter where we go, we take a little bit of each other everywhere." You see folks, there is no such thing as a self-made man or woman.

I have seen evil and misfortune in my life...and stared it down. Never could I have found the courage and resiliency to comeback, had it not been for others who experienced the ups and downs and twists and turns of their own pathways. Every story has its cast of characters. Most autobiographies include a special teacher, coach, mentor or significant friend that led their way. I am no different; however, the one character above all others is Jesus Christ. As my story unfolds, you'll note that I am not a Bible thumper. Nor am I a religious zealot or nut. As the saying goes, I do, however, subscribe to spiritual fruit.

Though I speak in my own voice, it is my prayer that God's Voice trumps my own as you read my story. May my story continue to capture the spirit of the times in which I am writing about, making you feel more connected to the story as you, too, reminisce the times of your life. It is my desire that every reader experience a visual montage, giving way to "the laughter and the tears, the shadows of misty yesteryears. The good times and the bad you've seen, and all the others in between." Many thanks to Canadian-born musician and performer Paul Anka for those beautifully written lyrics from his hit song of 1975 called *Times of Your Life*. As said, we all have a story. Mine is a bit out of the ordinary. I imagine many reading my story now feel the same way about their own story.

Memories and life are time-sensitive. All of us have moments when we reflect on our childhood, only to be riveted back to the present. In my first book, one of the two themes in *Your Pathway to Personal Enrichment & Vocational Enlightenment* was that of striking a balance between life at work and that at home (the other theme being the "forces of change"). Therefore, in writing my autobiography I have chosen to weave different "times of my life," toggling back and forth from childhood to adulthood...from my corporate life to my personal life. At times, I – like many others – felt as if I had two lives: The person at work and the guy at home.

Now – older, I am amazed at how God has used my life experiences to prepare me for the role as a life and career coach – "The Encourager." Whenever a crisis occurred, God was in control. Each crisis, on its own merit, would knock many of us off our game. Somehow, by the grace of God, I kept bouncing back. How people want to define their doctrine of choice is their business. I am not here to have a denominational battle on who has the best church. Let us just say the ecumenical part of my faith believes uncompromisingly that there is a God. He knows our prayers. That said, He makes a difference! To God goes the glory. Period. And – Amen!

Before we return to the rest of my story, I would like to share what two iconic figures have said about this thing we call "life." First, Robert Frost. He summed up life in three words by saying "…it goes on." I found that humorous, for multiple generations bridging both the 19th and 20th centuries, looking for infinite wisdom from one of the world's great poets. He kept it so simple. Secondly, there is the legendary evangelist Rev. Billy Graham. When asked by the popular talk show host Larry King about life, Graham simply replied with, "How fast it goes by." And so it does. Time, indeed moves on and it seems to move rather fast the older we get. Therefore, I tell my story the way we are: sometimes in the present, drawing and remembering from the past, and sometimes from the past, sharing the journey back to the present. Each with its Lessons Learned. I am fond of telling people I coach to not be prisoners of the past, but products of the past, yielding new opportunity and understanding.

As we return to my story it is my prayer that you experience an awakening-spirit, one that encourages you to look for the best in others, to build on what is good – all of which is God's way of revealing His grace to you through me.

FIRST CAREER CRISIS AND PERSONAL PASSAGES

Welcome back my friends to my victory march. But, before there can be a claim for victory we have to pick up the story from earlier, where I referred to a gathering storm building in my professional and personal life.

In World of Work: Growing Pains and Gains I wrote of my foster father's continuing criticisms and demands, together with the changing management scene at work.

In the mid to late 1970's I continued to love being a banker, always loyal to my employers – making them look good! No matter what I felt about a boss personally, my attitude was first shaped by a respect for their position. For that reason alone, I survived in my profession of first choice longer than most. While I was kissing their behinds and doing what was expected of me – plus more (always one to exceed expectations) – what I did not see was the humorous notion that the newcomers would easily make for great research material for the writers and producers of the classic cult movie *Office Space*, a comedy made two decades later, satirizing an American software company managed by a handful of buffoons. Just being honest.

Let me be clear. The bank was a world-class organization! I learned a lot from my experience gained at 127 Public Square, Cleveland, Ohio. The building was more than a 19th century landmark. It was a proud institution. It was a regional bank. But, as Dylan wrote and I've said more than once here, times were changing.

New technology was a force of change, making organizations

redefine the forces of management (planning, organizing, staffing, directing and control). The way banking products were traditionally marketed and delivered would require new strategies. Obviously, the board of directors felt our proud organization was ripe for new blood. So, they went outside the organization (outside the state for that matter), to recruit their change agents.

The new bosses were totally Machiavellian. An employee's loyalty or personal profile meant nothing to the new kids on the block. They were hired guns…hatchet men, if you will. At first, I was naïve. My lack of experience had not yet prepared me to recognize their cunning ways. I did, however, feel their wrath. Directives and guidance were meted out by military-like orders and commands! Asking a question was practically considered insubordination. Management pausing at your work station or office was unheard of during those times. One was summoned to their inner sanctum.

It befuddled me: How a proud organization with such rich origins and mission statements could evolve into just another ego-driven, merger-manic, profit-at-any-cost company. It was if we shed our banking skin. We were no longer money-changers, committed to our community. We had become some kind of a cog in a conglomerate wheel.

The new organizational behavior left an impact on my life for years to come, especially later in my career when I was an executive recruiter…and still later, a life and career coach. As one dismantles organizational structures, looking past the material aspects of brick and mortar, it always comes back to PEOPLE! The managers who had once been my mentors – absolute experts and leaders in their field and community – were being relegated to other positions by means of lateral transfers (or else). The word "ruthless" comes to mind. Looking back, it reminded me of Milton, the "stapler guy" in *Office Space*, who systematically was being eased out of his various roles, eventually having his desk – and stapler – relocated in the company basement. Sometimes humor and satire can make a great point! Sadly, the satire works because it reflects reality.

Work was no longer fun. It was not as rewarding as it was during my first several years with the bank. Nonetheless, it paid the bills. My first career crisis was brewing, but my life was about to experience a personal passage that would change my life forever!

A Victory March

Connie

Connie and I were introduced to one another by the same family that introduced me to my friend Dave Hach. My high school friend who invited me to tag along for a golfing vacation in Myrtle Beach, South Carolina had a brother. He (Bob) was married to a teacher who happened to teach with Connie, seventy miles away from Cleveland (Mansfield, Ohio). Now that you have some of those dots connected, allow me to tell you the story within the story. Connie Ann Clemann knew about me, as I did her, for the better part of two years (through our mutual friends).

She was raised in Iowa, where she knew from a very young age that she wanted to become a teacher. She had lost her father to cancer. Her mom met another gentleman who also lost his spouse to cancer. In recent years I've learned how such a personal loss feels. Her mom and the other gentleman, each with children, became their own version of television's family *The Brady Bunch*. When Connie was a senior in high school her mother was pregnant. For the record, I never heard any of the six children or parents reference the word "step." Jokingly, the parents referred to their children as "hers, his and ours." Connie worked many jobs, putting herself through college. Following college, she and her roommate began their careers in education in Mansfield, Ohio.

As said, for two years we learned a lot about one another from our two mutual friends. I knew of her personal loss. I also appreciated hearing of her moral and spiritual convictions. Connie enjoyed bowling and playing tennis. She liked – correct that – LOVED chocolate. She had more shoes than the rather famous Philippines First Lady Imelda Marcos, who allegedly had several thousand pairs! We liked the same kind of music and food. Importantly, we shared common philosophies. She collected "Precious Moments" figurines. I had a Mickey Mouse collection. We both loved Disney movies and characters. She had a kick-butt impression of Donald Duck (forgive me honey). I had Ed Sullivan down better than Ed Sullivan had himself. You see, we both had a sense of humor.

Connie was an independent professional woman. She was a beautiful woman. She knew of my beliefs and professional ambitions, though I restrained from elaborating at great length all my personal history from her. After all, I didn't want to scare her away. We had a blind date – two years in the making. She figured she had nothing lose and every reason to enjoy a well-done petite steak at Adam's Rib restaurant.

We met, despite her mailing me a card with errant directions (I still have the evidence). It was meant to be – to meet. We met under the soft accent lights showcasing full-figured nude women of the Renaissance years. For years I would embellish our first meeting with stories about that evening. Of course, I would exaggerate (the art of comedy) the number of naked pictures, errant directions and so forth. I would often tell of the lovely Sunday school teacher that took me to a restaurant of her choice that featured pictures of naked women. Forgive me reader. I am alone these day, my wife taken by a cruel disease. Memories are all I have left of her. If she was in our conversation here, she would join in our laughter over bare-naked ladies – which for some odd reason remains riveted on my mind. I best move on.

It was love at first sight. Just like the movies. We knew much about one another by the time we met. She was everything I was looking for in a woman, especially since I had fears that if I ever married, my life would be cut short from a cancer relapse. It would take a strong woman to care for children, should I pass on. As a teacher, she would go back to work when the children would be of school age. Summers, spring breaks and Christmas, along with other holidays would be set aside for family time. It was a perfect match for "life [style] and career."

I proposed one month after our blind date. We were married April 17, 1976 six months after our autumn date. True to our mutually agreed upon style, we had a simple wedding with a reception at the church where she taught Sunday school. It was the day before Easter. And, blessedly, our day was graced by uncommonly warm spring weather. Several years later, when taking writing and communication classes at a local college, an assignment was given to write a descriptive one-page piece on an "important event" in our lives. The professor allotted twenty minutes!

Because I still honor my wife's personal preferences, I am cautious and conservative about what I share in this book about her. Eventually, her life-threatening illness became a part of this story. I believe I have struck the proper balance of sharing a story that needs told, while not compromising her wishes. For the moment, below is what I wrote during my twenty minute writing assignment:

A Victory March
Memories of a Special Wedding Day

People were filling the sanctuary. The next hour would bring happiness, tears of joy and fulfillment.

Meanwhile, the bride, Connie, was sharing precious moments with her mother. Her bridesmaid, Terri, was equally involved with her sister's final moments of single life. On the other side of the church confines was the groom, John. He was moved by the overwhelming response to the wedding invitations, as he peered through the cracks of the double doors. Before leaving the private room, John and his best man, Dave, shared a brief prayer.

A mild and mellow melody of love filled the church; the sonorous harmony between the guitar and the groom's vocal chords left the invited audience touched by the beautiful ballad known as *And I Love You So*. There was a misty gleam in the eyes of the bride. Silly as it may have seemed, it looked like she didn't know whether to laugh or to cry.

Many of the guest, some as far away as Oregon and New York, were deep in thought and reflection. There was, for instance, the bride's younger brother Steven. Little did he know the next few years would yield a nephew named in his honor…that his own life would discover the same matrimonial bliss…and how the groom and himself would become lifelong friends. Then there was Mr. and Mrs. Thompson and Mr. and Mrs. Klein, the parents of the bride and groom, perhaps recalling moments from their past when wedding bells chimed and vows were exchanged.

Pastor Duncan, bespectacled, was young and scholarly looking. Because the bride was one of his own church family, he took special pride in this blessed event.

****

Connie and I were married for thirty-six years as husband and wife, mother and father. We were a team. She was my partner and companion for life. I could write you volumes about her, but as indicated above, will be restrictive due to her being a very private person. I will do my best to obligate the story without compromising her wishes. Obviously, Connie was a huge part of my new life.

Together, we faced catastrophic long-term illness – a crisis by anyone's definition – during the last several years of her life. Connie was with me when experiencing our first crisis, one that was a career crisis. And that is where we'll pick up the story.

Connie was a stay home mom, taking care of our two sons – one adopted and one conceived by natural birth (premature as he was). It was my turn to be a husband and father. The contrast between my manner and that of my foster father could not have been more different. My foster parents – now being grandparents – became very demanding and out-spoken. Obviously, tension grew within our family ranks. Connie was getting initiated into my world.

Connie and I were more than gracious with making time for our children to have some quality time with their grandparents, especially since the maternal grandparents were far away in Oregon. My foster parents would argue with us on matters of child-rearing, including our dietary choices, shots and sleeping habits. All grandchildren get spoiled a bit, but we're not talking about minor issues. Without too much elaboration, one son would tell me in recent years of food being forced down his throat, "whether he liked it or not" (a sickening reminder of my own ordeal as a child). Our older son was taken on a snowmobile without being secured. His winter clothing got caught in the rotating blades. Thank God the engine choked and stalled! Grandfather barked that it was "no big deal."

We wanted my parents to have a relationship with their grandchildren, but my foster mom would relapse often from her cancer battles. Regardless, they became more outspoken about what they deemed were "parental shortcoming" in Connie and myself. No doubt, at night during family devotion time, I was prone to sarcastically say to my enlightened wife, "Welcome to my family honey."

All this, while going back to work every morning, only to hear a boss rant uncontrollably about demands he couldn't put into words. His temperament was all too familiar with me. Immediate supervisors and managers in the reporting stream were being reassigned. I should have been delighted! I had been promoted to Customer Service Officer at the parent company headquarters! I had achieved a goal – a dream! I was a graduate of Solon High School, believing I made something out of myself – when most looked upon me as a hardship case, likely not going to win the aforementioned "most likely to succeed" award.

Quite the opposite, actually. My foster father should be proud of me, I thought – wrongly. He hardly acknowledged my accomplishment.

I was summoned to their home in Solon one night after work,

following a death in my foster father's family. There was an estate. My foster father's words were, "You're the big shot banker! Get on the phone and figure this out!" Clue: There was a modest inheritance involved, yielding a modest split among ten family members. I talked and faked my way through the process, netting my foster father approximately $100 dollars (which he likely would have gotten without my help). He just assumed because I was a banker (though on the non-credit side of the business), that I was comparable to a lawyer in the legal field. Surely, in his mind, it meant that I must also be a Trust Officer! I can laugh at it now; but, at the time, that man would have nearly killed me or anyone else to get what he considered his "just due" (even if only $100 dollars). I would listen to rants and raves – a diatribe – on how "deserving" he was of his rightful inheritance. I dare not challenge him during such moments. His eyes would flair and his fist would coil. He was an angry man. And, once again, I was smack in the middle of his anger.

The same strange dilemma persisted at work: Being in the way of someone's anger! Life was not fun. And through it all my foster mother was deathly ill and deeply dispirited. The tug-of-war was stressful: Play it safe at work, becoming a pawn or pigeon expected to fill any hole available or risk the job market, looking for adventure. Play it safe at home, becoming a person that met other people's expectations (foster parents) more than the needs of my own family.

An opportunity was available in central Ohio, what some might call becoming a big fish in a small pond. Going from a parent company to an autonomous affiliate community bank was a big risk! But it would test my mettle. While the title of Chief Operating Officer is impressive sounding, more importantly it is a test of leadership – no matter what the scope of the operation might be. It is a lot of responsibility. I had people encouraging me to make the leap. And I did!

Lesson learned? Euphoria may wear off, whether it be in the workplace or at home. But discouragement does not last, so long as we keep to our principles. Above all – that means staying faithful to God's purposes. Eventually, sacrifice and conflict give way to success. Pursuing that pathway may mean weathering the setbacks. It means learning patience. It means learning what the founder of modern medicine, Hippocrates, wrote long ago: "Life is short. The art is long." I learned that I still had a lot to learn about life.

The home I grew up in. Solon, Ohio

A telling picture, taken after my catechism class at St. Rita's where my spiritual awakening began. Much later, I eulogized my foster father, remembering him as an "Individualist." He was also indifferent.

7th grade: A brutal year, one that nearly broke my spirit – at home and at school.

I had a lot on my mind in high school. The brood mood. The basketball became an instrument in building self-esteem.

My first car, on the farm.

This was my brief stint as a ventriloquist with longtime friend Bobby Z. This picture was taken shortly after moving out of the foster home. I had a lot to smile about!

I enjoyed entertaining my friends!

A Victory March

Connie and I were a great team.

We marched to victory together.

My Best Decision Ever!
April 17, 1976

1979 – Steven laughing, Doug plotting, Connie dreaming, me enjoying!

Comedian Bill Cosby once called children "a sexually transmitted disease." Hardly! They brought me pure joy… still do.

There were many a sleepover in the Klein household.

Dad and sons

Steve and Doug

Sons, Steven and Doug.
They grew up.

The Legendary head covers that were exchanged every Christmas!

Ed "Iron" Hach and Momma Hach.
The funniest and the smartest!

Dave and Beverly Hach

October 11, 1997 Mr. and Mrs. Hach ask me to sing *And I Love You So* at their 50th Wedding Anniversary.

At Steve and Tracy's wedding reception. Smiles all around!

Apache Junction boat ride with my wife.

Son, Daughter-in-law and Grandchildren

With my golfing buddy and best swing coach ever,

Nick Wahl

With my friend and great writer,

Colin Comerford

Mr. and Mrs. Hach 60th Wedding Anniversary. What a Blessing!

2007

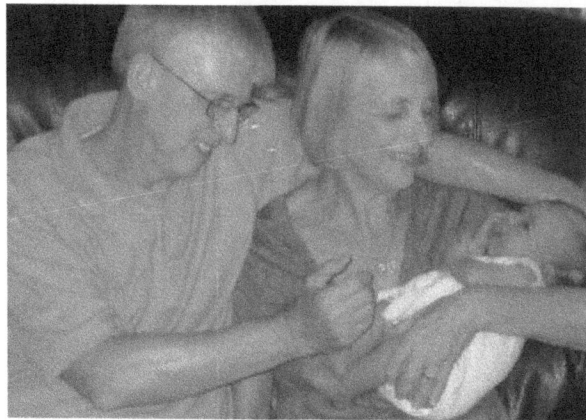

The "money shot," as my son calls it. "Staying in the moment," Got Connie to this precious moment, without a doubt, my finest coaching.

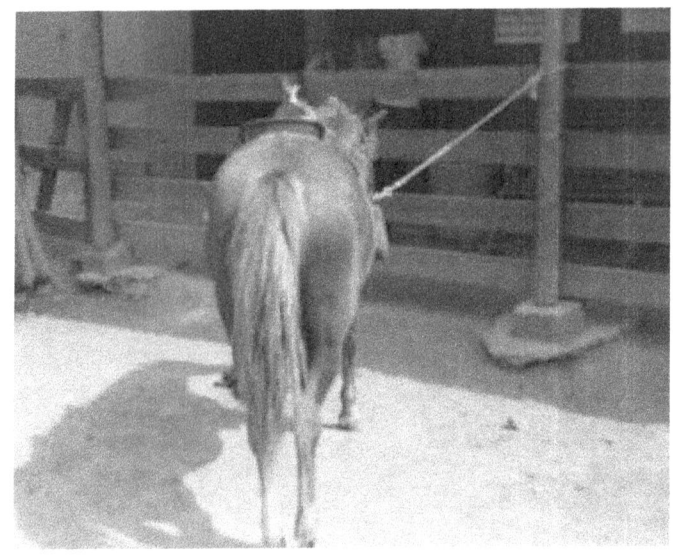

From the world of work: when working in the public sector, a Government job, I felt as if this is who I worked for.

WORLD OF WORK: BANKING LEAVES ME

When former California governor Ronald Reagan switched his party affiliation from that of a democrat to a republican he was fond of saying, "The Democratic Party left me, I didn't leave them." That is how I viewed my banking career. For four years my bank president in central Ohio gave me all the rope I wanted so long as I used it wisely. I did. He was a very popular community leader and one of the best people I ever reported to in the workplace. He was recognized nationally as one of the youngest and most successful bankers in the country. It was a blessing to have his confidence. Having said that, he walked a fine line with the board of directors and executive staff, for having hired a guy from the outside (now it was I that wore the Outsider's label) – except, unlike the software hires mentioned earlier (Cleveland), I actually was a banker.

I also looked like I was barely pubescent. I looked like the Doogie Howser of the banking world. As mentioned elsewhere, once I solved problems, my appearance mattered little to my adversaries and skeptics. It was a lesson learned. I made my boss and my staff look good. Somehow, it all made me look better too, taking me almost all of the four years I served in that senior management role to gain the respect and acceptance of my peers (at least those that were home grown, if you will). My role not only included being head of operations, it included business development and corporate services. Proudly, our affiliate bank introduced account analysis services to our business customers. We made it possible for the bank to know its profitability customer-by-customer, likewise making it possible for that customer to know its excess funds availability (thus retaining their services from being pirated by competitors – of which there were many). The parent company (flagship bank) in the holding company would turn to our affiliate to test market new financial products and services. They had confidence in our first-class operation and we were known for our organizational development.

In any event, the law of unintended consequences, more or less, evolved into a role involving me more and more with the cash management division out of Columbus, Ohio. My hats were varied: Operations Management, Customer Service, Business Development and Corporate Services/Cash Management. Walking on water was not required, but I did have many masters. Organizational structure and flow charts were hardly realistic. On paper, they were confusing. In real life, they were nothing less than scripts for creating clashes between good people within the organization.

For instance, a branch manager, understandably, does not want to report to an operations man or woman. When it came to cross-selling corporate services and providing support and training to the credit side of the bank, it is an uncomfortable role for someone on the non-credit side (operations) to direct the process. Branch managers were accustomed to having a straight reporting line on an organizational chart, not some indirect reporting path (dotted line) by way of operations. The parent company kept me busy with training and selling expectations, while the affiliate would have me putting out local fires. The role had out-grown itself. And I was growing tired of the intramural politics and butt-kissing required between the competing and ill-structured lines of authority. For me to remain in banking it was becoming clear that I would have to relocate a few times over the next few years.

Banking was about to leave me. It was okay. I was bored with sales quotas, baby-sitting and organizational cliques (that go with living in a smaller community).

I LOVED BEING A FATHER

Our children were out of diapers. They were involved in school and they worshipped their mommy and daddy. An iconic, nationally known comedian reminded every parent and child in America that marriage and parenting could be humorous. There is a magic time when our children experience the "wonder years," which fade too soon. Bill Cosby made a living making parents and kids alike laugh hysterically. Being one that looks for the best in others, I dared to include his name when writing this book. It is sad to hear of recent allegations of this great comedian, but I'll leave those matters to others for another day. For now, what remains is a lifetime of work dedicated to helping families laugh at themselves. He made us look at the lighter side of family growing pains, rather than be preoccupied with violence. Our family was growing up. We always had a household of young people staying in our home. I now felt like one of the parents like those described in Families of Another Name.

It was pure joy opening our home to other kids in the neighborhood or from school. Without embarrassing anyone, I too, was becoming a surrogate father. I had to be careful to not let my own children feel left behind or slighted. I accepted the role for all it was worth. It was my turn to pay forward.

While laughter filled our home during the autumn of 1983, sorrow overcame our joy on August 23rd – to be exact. For months I had been commuting to and from the Cleveland Area from my home in central Ohio. My foster mother needed care. My foster father wasn't about to change his ways. I would visit her cancer-ridden body, sadly one with a broken spirit. It was incredibly depressing. After personal care needs were attended to, I would sit and talk with her. Honestly, it didn't help much. Yet, before I would leave, each and every time, she would take my hand, stare straight into my eyes, saying, "Johnny, I don't want to die alone." Grace was my guide. Brother Richard, to his credit, stayed in Solon, briefly to lend assistance during her last weeks. Eventually, she needed more hospitalization. The family was told it would likely be weeks before the cancer would take its toll. If my own wife was alive, Connie would attest to this incredible truth: In bed, that fateful night of August 23rd, I turned to my wife – weeks before my foster mother's expected passing – telling my wife that I had to leave for Cleveland – to be with my foster mom (so that she not be alone).

There was no audible voice. No set agenda by doctors and nurses. Just intuition? It was inexplicable. I did what had to be done, honoring my foster mother's last wish – to not die alone. I barely made it to the hospital in time. The nurses would check her vital signs, looking at me sympathetically, urging me to go home (Mr. Klein, it could be weeks yet...please go home and get some rest). The experts were wrong. Fifteen minutes before my foster mother's last breath, she told me a story of a woman that would come to visit me during my childhood.

Recalling those visits, I acknowledged her weak, rambling message. For whatever reason, Mary E. Klein wanted me to know that visitor – whom I was always told was a "social worker" – was really my biological mother! My foster mother then placed a small, folded newspaper clipping in my hand. It was the last thing, other than my hand that she held. The article was about a lady, living elsewhere in Ohio, having won a contest. She had a government job. That is all I will say about it, as I believe her name, picture and details should remain as my birth mother would have likely preferred: Private. For sure, it was a strange encounter. Mother Mary was not speaking words of wisdom, but I let it be. It hurt like hell. It hurt more deeply because my foster mother felt so inadequate with her own motherhood. She felt compelled to drop an unbelievable bombshell on me – on her own death bed! I wondered alone in my thoughts on how she knew I was coming to the hospital. I had not called in advance. She just knew. I choose to belief it had something to do with faith and grace (that her foster son would honor her final wish to not die alone).

Emotionally, I was spent the night my foster mother died in my arms. Not just because of the obvious, but because she wanted me to know my real (biological) mother loved me (enough to give me up) – though my foster mom could not muster a few remaining breaths – just once in her life – that she loved me too. It was all so surreal, like a dark soap opera. When notifying my foster father of his loss, he blamed me for "killing her." I am not making that up. My presence, he claimed, gave her reason to not live anymore. It came as no surprise to me. After all, weeks earlier, while my foster mother – his wife – was in surgery, he went to an automotive repair shop to replace the muffler on his car. He left any communications and/or decisions with the doctors to me. On the night of her death, he left her final arrangements in my hands as well. Honest to God, I don't know how the man slept at night. Thank God – her hands were in my hands, too. It struck me: During her waning breaths, hand in hand, a life with one last request – a destiny we all must take – that one final moment would be that of saying goodbye to one mother, while saying hello to another, albeit silently.

Lesson learned was that not only was life short and artful, it is interesting. People who find life dull are dull. So I avoid them. I learned that enthusiasm is a healthy emotion; yet, it can be dampened by the loss of a loved one, especially one that you sought love from in return. Such loss produces a different kind of pain than one that has pleasant memories. It is because of what could have been or should have been. It leaves a hole in our soul when love is denied by life's depravities and debasement. My foster mother deserved a better fate. Her life was defined by the poor choosing of a mate.

Another lesson learned was that memories count. My foster mother loved the farm. And she loved her miniature kerosene lamp collection (Lord, she had more than four hundred of them). Every now and then, just being simple-minded, while amusing myself, I would read by candlelight. Books never rejected me or denied me the fountain of knowledge contained within them. From George Bernard Shaw there was this beautiful quote: "Life is no brief candle to me. It is a sort of splendid torch which I have got to hold for the moment, and I want to make it burn as brightly as possible before handing it on to future generations." Three decades later a "hope candle" would become my vigil for my wife Connie, as cancer would claim her too. I have said goodbye to two women where a candle had symbolism for each. Both women still live in my heart, just different chambers. And the flame will never be extinguished. I loved them both. But, only one had a reply from the first verse of *And I Love You So* (…and I love you too…). A postscript to the meaning of this can be taken from my first book, *Your Pathway to Personal Enrichment & Vocational Enlightenment*, whereby I cite an author unknown, saying, "You cannot hold a torch to light another's path without brightening your own." Accordingly, for most my life, despite hardships, I rarely walked in the dark.

Sometimes the shadows would follow me – as depicted in my favorite ballad. I had plenty of critics offering their unsolicited commentaries on how I blew off a promising banking career. Yet, always there were other people that carried a torch, brightening my pathway. While not yet old, I tried to be the "Old Lamplighter" – a character described in my foster mother's favorite song of the same name. Elton John could have his candle in the wind.

So, I figured I could have my torch and lamplight. The lamplight was the logo for my company, Kleinmark, LLC. I am an 'encourager' because I was called to be a lamplighter unto the world. It started as a boy, giving comfort to my foster mother when she needed light. Till I take my last breath, I will hold that torch for others, only blessing my own life through and through. An Encourager am I, before it was my brand. A lamplighter was I the day my foster mother said goodbye with one last squeeze of my hand.

John J. Klein

****

My banking career and foster mother now part of my past, life went on in Mansfield, Ohio. A career shift was underway, Connie was teaching as usual and kids were doing what kids do: Grow! As our boys got older we got busier. Soon, the word "coach" would become part of my identity. A youth organization in town – The Johnny Appleseed League – was looking for an expansion team. My youngest son wanted to play baseball and I was ready to be his coach (not to mention what so many fathers tend to do: Vicariously live out their dreams through their children). Indeed, I became the coach. And my son Doug would become a pitcher. He had natural talent, but had a lot to learn – like dad! Being the rookie coach, I learned quickly about the practice of old-timer coaches handpicking the best talent – loading their teams, so to speak (human nature, I supposed). One such team was coached by an imposing fellow I wanted to beat so bad my lips bled. It was like a made-for-television show. As mentioned, I had a lot to learn. I fell prey to the oldest trick in baseball: The double steal from first base and third. Boy oh' boy, that one stung. It caught me off guard, as it did, of course, the kids. The first time that ploy was played on our team, it cost us the game! I never forgot that strategy, though – at the time – it seemed dirty and sneaky. It wasn't. It was a smart tactic. The more experienced coach taught me a lesson. Like parenting, coaching is not for wimps.

A lesson learned was that there is a difference between envy and jealousy. The little league experience revealed a character flaw that needed some work. I was jealous of the opposing team's coach, for having the wherewithal and craftiness to beat me. During an evening devotion, God reminded me that my little league team was not about me. I missed an opportunity to teach my team a lesson (which later I did). That is to say, that jealousy is when we want to deny another what they have. I was wrong to be jealous of the other coach and his handpicked loaded team. He wanted to win! Don't we all? Envy is when we simply "want" what someone else has (what is working for them). When we learn the difference between jealousy and envy we learn about humility. When we learn humility, we learn what it takes to be a winner. Meanwhile, when not playing and coaching America's favorite pastime – baseball, I was recreating my career path. The voices of my critics played in my head (especially when bills were due). What was I thinking? Why did I leave my banking profession, my passion of first choice? Frankly, I did not miss the action. I was not ego-driven and I did not feel as if I failed in my corporate life.

Sometime titles are like toilets. They come in different sizes, shapes and forms. Some fit. Some don't. I enjoyed my new job – working for an executive search firm. Job-seekers and hiring authorities alike were looking. It was a busy job market. Companies were paying handsome fees when it came to executive placements. The firm I joined was franchised. It had an absentee owner, who gladly allowed me to use my management experience to hold down the office. Of course, my primary function would be to recruit candidates that would make him money. I made him look good. We verbally agreed that upon his forthcoming retirement that I would buy the franchise from him at an agreed upon price.

Two years later – with no one else billing placements – he was ready to sell…for TWICE the originally agreed upon price! His rationale? I had doubled the number of placements from the previous year; thus, he felt it was fair to double the asking price of the franchise. Go figure. We parted company as amiably as possible and I satisfied my entrepreneurial itch by starting my first company out of my home: The J. J. Klein Company. Original, eh?

It was an executive recruiting firm specializing in the banking field (where I still had many contacts from more seminars and meetings than I care to remember). For five years I had life on my terms. I would take my family on vacations, including exciting places like Disney World and alternating visits with the in-laws in Oregon. Eventually the economy would slow. Executive recruitment was feeling more like flesh peddling (not my cup of tea). I did more resume writing and career coaching than I did placements. Though rewarding at times, it did not pay the bills. Little did I know, however, how useful those acquired skills would become later in my life. My family was growing. So were their appetites! I needed a steadier job with more income and benefits to provide for my family. It was time to abandon my stint as an entrepreneur. Maybe banking had not left me after all.

Lesson learned was that some things we should get in writing. A verbal agreement between my hero Arnold Palmer and his attorney friend Mark McCormack was not going to work for me.

WORLD OF WORK: BLUE COLLAR TIME

The J.J. Klein Company was in my rear view mirror. As said in closing my last chapter, the requisite for more income was commensurate with the growing needs of my family. Our children had a penchant for wanting to help others. Hmmm. I wonder where they learned that from. Ours was an open home, where kids from the neighborhood or school were always welcomed. There were always extra mouths to feed. The pull-out couch was used often to accommodate overnight guest. At times the sleeping bags strewn about the family room floor looked much like fish washed up on the beach. It was pure joy! Connie and I loved having the kids in our home. After all, God was now using our home to help others, at times, the way "families of another name" helped me.

Legendary Ohio State football coach, Woody Hayes, called such benevolence "paying forward." Often, it had nothing to do with being altruistic; we just made our home a popular place for young people to hang out. A favorite meal in our household was spaghetti (déjà vu). The range of activities would vary from basketball, baseball, golf and the silliness of WWF (World Wrestling Federation with the likes of Andre the Giant and Hulk Hogan).

I wish I had been a bodybuilder like the aforementioned wrestling icons. It would have served me well for the short several month stint I had as a steelworker. You heard me right! I learned the hard way that going back into the business world was harder than expected, especially when the economy is slow and economic development goes south from your geographic area. My neighbor happened to be a union leader. We could not have been more different: He – very liberal. Me – more conservative. I could go into more differences, but you get the idea.

Remember, grace is my guide. As different as we were, we respected one another. I introduced him to golf. And that was my saving grace with having him as a neighbor. We would practice pitch shots in the front yard, when I was not throwing footballs or baseballs to my kids and their friends. He would argue with me about anything, building his case for anything or everything that defined itself diametrically opposed to my way of thinking. It was crazy. Yet, we got along. Why? Because we were honest with one another. And we respected the enormous responsibilities that each of us had carried with us on the job. He knew my community reputation and how hardworking I was and I knew how involved he was representing thousands of people who at one time or another experienced job injustice or labor-management issues. Like me, he earned his dues. That work ethic was our subordinate point of agreement. It made for a healthy, neighborly relationship despite our many differences personally, spiritually, politically and socially.

Due to our common ground he came to my rescue, making it possible for me to re-enter the local workforce. Working at the steel mill meant it would be necessary for me to start at the ground floor (literally). The starting positions were floor man and gauger. In other words, entry-level.

Once oriented into the plant, I would apply for a management position, perhaps manufacturing sales or human resources. Seemed like a good idea at the time. It was not! Because of my "white collar" reputation, the union faithful spread rumors that I was not a "working man" or that I was likely being trained to be a "foreman" (a job grade comparable to being Satan). Though a few who knew me well considered my genesis from a senior banking position to pushing pigeon dung around a plant floor was a fall from grace, I chose to see it as a passage with grace. I was determined to learn from the experience.

It prepared me well for what would come later in life. I can tell you this: It was a very diverse work ethic. I understand union solidarity, but not when it comes to protecting militants, saboteurs and loafers. I saw too much. Humbly, I pushed that pigeon dung – trying to remind myself that I was doing God's work. Managing a crisis, hiring and developing a staff and meeting budgets seemed remote to me as I performed the common job in an uncommon way. I got paid well to push that broom and gauge that steel. I did not complain. I made my boss look good. By the way, he really was a good guy. He knew my personal circumstances and respected me for doing a good day's work. My union brethren and co-workers were hardly as nice. I was threatened and mocked just about every day on the job. I figured it would pass. It never did. I made a few friends, but few and far between - remembering the sage advice my neighbor gave me months earlier: "John, if you cannot make any friends, don't make enemies."

For all the differences we had with one another that was great advice! Unfortunately, it did not serve me well in a field where "I did not fit in." Working a double shift (great money) was physically demanding. I was a small fellow and I never told anyone about my arm. It was incredible that I lasted as long as I did. I should have filed for worker's compensation, but my pride kept me from doing the right thing. I just quit (which is not my nature). It was not my best "operating mode" (as we say in life coaching and skill assessment). I "did not belong." Had I been more patient, likely a front office position would have been available to me. Patience with others is an asset with me. Patience with myself is another matter.

Before I hang up my blue collar chapter, let me end it with a quick anecdotal story for comic relief. Earlier I mentioned the WWF. My kids were huge fans of this nonsensical, scripted, fake wrestling….entertainment. My wife and I would foolishly spend pay-per-view cable fees. We would alternate these ridiculous social dramas between our house and that of a school principal we knew in our school system. He was a fairly large fellow – compared to my slight frame. He and I colluded to secretly raid one of the telecast, dressed in WWF-like garb.

We planned on pummeling our young'uns into submission, burying them in couch cushions until they cried for mercy. On this occasion the event was at the principals house (a nice upper-middle class neighborhood). I was dressed in tight shorts, while wearing a wife-beater shirt, bandana, war paint and carrying a whip in my hand (which was among many gags I used when managing operations at the bank). It was a well thought out costume. I arrived as stealthily as possible, precisely on time. My cohort in crime met me at his front door, yelling that his wife was home and that we were about to have a lot of fun! He might have yelled something goofy, like – "LET'S RUMBLE!" Steps away a neighbor was mowing an adjacent strip of grass next to the driveway I was standing on, while trying to look fierce (having my game face, if you will). The look on his neighbor's face was priceless! I do believe we – for a few moments – gave the good neighbor the wrong idea. Kids will be kids.

Lessons learned were significant. I learned to "apply" what I lived and learned (later used in my first book). Learning that "if I couldn't make friends, don't make enemies" was worthwhile. All modesty aside, I learned that I was one tough son of a gun! Trust me people, most steelworkers (even the loafers) earn their money. It is hard work! I learned how to better set aside personal bias and prejudice, to favor clear-thinking principles.

My family needed me to provide for them. Twice – this being the first – I would find myself in mid-career having worked a job that, frankly, I hated. Of course, I drew upon my principle thinking, knowing I had food to put on the table and bills to pay. My character was being tested. So was my faith. I learned how much I missed my "profession of first choice – Banking!"

Missing banking was not just a lesson learned from not working at the bank or because of the sweat and toil of grinding it out in a steel mill. No, it was more because of the lessons learned at a church ministered by a former athlete hailing from a high school sports conference (The Chagrin Valley Conference). Dave was a competing rival, a gifted star basketball player for Chagrin Falls. He would call me Comet (our team logo/mascot). I would call him Tiger. As you might have guessed, Dave was the senior pastor of our church. Our Sunday school program featured a series from a popular mid-1980's financial advisor, Larry Burkett. Mr. Burkett proved to be quite prophetic about my generation's over-consumption and our willingness to place debt on the backs of our children.

I began to embrace much of what the author preached. For the record (this isn't the forum to go deep on the subject), I disagreed with him on Keynesian Economic theory and policy. At times I believe the Central Bank (The Federal Reserve) has a role to control the money supply and to exercise regulatory oversight. We live in a mixed socio-economic capitalistic system that must co-exist in a global marketplace. Reading and hearing Burkett's series reminded me of my roots in banking. Remember: Books are my friends. I had read Dr. Paul Nadler's *Banking Jungle*. He was an esteemed expert in the financial field and the banking industry. Between the two of those authors – I wanted back in the action! One problem: No one was hiring! I applied everywhere. I came close, that is, if my wife and I wanted to wine and dine commercial customers every month. High Society was not our style. Besides, it also meant relocating. I was having some health concerns and we did not want to give up Connie's top of the scale continuing contract status from teaching. Her profession was a major anchor to our stability. Suddenly, Connie had become the breadwinner! But, irresponsible debt (just as Mr. Burkett warned) made it necessary for two incomes. I had to pull my weight. Though I can claim that banking left me, it had me begging for another chance to jump back in the game. But those doors did not open.

My entrepreneurial stint had run its course. I needed to be needed. Then one day an opportunity presented itself in stark contrast to the private sector. I was told there was a need for my talent in the public sector.

In the next chapter you will learn about the makings of my second career crisis. It meant working a job that kept me underemployed for twelve years. Having said that – to be fair – it provided good income for my family. It also afforded me more time at home with my family than any other job (including being self-employed).

The lesson about to be learned was that of my making the best of a job that offered broken promises from politicians and bureaucrats. My administrative experience was woefully ignored. Said promises were nothing but carrots and manure. Strange as it sounds, no one cared. Yes, I was about to learn all about politics (a field, in my youth, that I once thought to be honorable).

WORLD OF WORK: PUBLIC SECTOR
(TWELVE YEAR WAR AND SECOND CAREER CRISIS)

Sometimes we get hired for the wrong reason.

My ego was fed. Flattery seasoned with arsenic, as I call it. An outgoing county commissioner met with me, saying, "John, your considerable experience in the private sector is exactly what is needed in the public sector." He went on about my banking background, especially my training in financial control, with spread sheets and personnel development. I had taken to heart and mind Dr. Orlando Behling's *Diagnostic Approach*, (informative coursework from Ohio State University). A community college enhanced my continuing education, especially in communications, economics and management. My practical experience from two of the most profitable banks in the country, together with my continuing education didn't hurt my credentials. It made for an impressive interview.

Added value was the three Ohio Civil Service Exams I readily passed as a "walk-in" (at the request of a local politician). Passing those exams qualified me as a Personnel Officer (1, 2 and 3) for any county in Ohio! Simply put, they were a waste of time, except for the pride I might take in myself. My future employers ignored their merit, as they did my management experience. As time went by, I wondered why the heck they hired me. Like I said, I was about to learn all about politics.

One interview would lead to another interview. My career transitioned from the private sector to entrepreneurialism to the public sector. Woe be me: a government employee – like my wife. It all seemed so right at the time. Hours, benefits and opportunity. It was the worst career decision I ever made! But God's Grace made it the best lesson learned! Let me tell you the rest of the story.

I left my initial interview feeling needed. Had Abraham Maslow lived beyond 1970 he might have amended his theories on satisfying basic needs, whereby he advanced theories about lower level needs being met before realizing higher ones, such as self-actualization. Life can be abrupt – even cruel – at times, because of personal issues, job changes and a myriad of other forces (Years later, I would write about those "forces" in my book, *Your Pathway*). More often, however, change is brought on by legislative, regulatory, environmental, judicial, economic, cultural, current events, social or political forces. DID I BOLD TYPE POLITICAL? Ha! Trust me. Unless you've worked for the government, if you think politics doesn't rule, you're as naïve as I once was. Maslow believed that every desirable person was capable of climbing the mythical hierarchy of an organization: the ladder of success, if you will. Damn Maslow! Fact is: Making progress often means going backwards to go forwards (falling forward).

This has been especially true for the more recent workforce of this era, who are forced to take jobs beneath their desire and/or skill-level because that is all that is available in the scarce job market. Such was the case for me in 1989. I had mouths to feed and needed to keep the roof over our heads. "The mass of men live lives of quiet desperation," wrote Henry Thoreau. I was desperate.

So, back to the story. I was feeling needed, right? You have felt the same way, I'm sure. Well, we are both probably guilty of conceding the age-old quip, "If I knew then what I know now!" As for me, I would have known that I was being used like a lowly pawn in a chess game.

Every time I hear Sinatra's song, *That's Life*, (also sung more recently by Michael Buble), I think of the lyrics: "I've been a puppet, a pauper, a pirate, a poet, a pawn and a king…I've been up and down…over and out…and I know one thing…each time I find myself, flat on my face, I pick myself up and get back in the race…That's life…that's what all the people say…"

The rat race of life doesn't really bother me; I just hate it when the rats are winning! And I am here to tell you there's a lot rats in political circles. And yes – that's life! I just wish I had learned that lesson earlier in the University of Life. Those rats put my family through a lot of hell. And I have earned the right to write about it!

I was referred to another community leader who was quite popular in Central Ohio. He had strong connections in the business community, government agencies and academic circles. He was a force in his own right. He had left a position at a local vocational school, where I once had an interest in teaching an adult education class. He was very active in local politics. For the record, he was a Republican. At that time, I was a registered Republican (Today I am an Independent, what once I considered to be a fence walker. But, given the lack of problem solving by our legislative branch of government, I don't encourage either party anymore. They have to earn my vote now.) Anyway, the dude liked me.

As a former recruiter I can tell you, when it's all said and done, that's why most people get hired: likability. When meeting this gentleman that I was mildly acquainted with through other channels, we established instant rapport. We were both on our games. Ostensibly, we had what the other wanted. I was told the county needed my management training and banking skills. The county was developing a "workfare" program (another government funded jobs program that was more about the government creating jobs for themselves than for job seekers). The program would need a leader. Promises were implied. I'll give the gentleman the benefit of the doubt. Remember, I was desperate.

By the way, it was a blessing in disguise that the jobs program role never came to fruition, as I have strong personal beliefs on the merits (or lack of) of these government programs. Suffice to say, there's a few success stories. All too often, however, it is more about people who were not truly motivated to work. People will disagree. I'm just telling you that's my qualified opinion. I say qualified because I was part of the system and saw how it did not work.

Eventually, I found myself sitting in the Executive Director's office at Human Services. It was 1989. The interview process was coming to a close, leading to a hire. I felt so happy – for my family! The office theme was adorned by pictures and symbols featuring the life of Abraham Lincoln. I was getting a feel for my interviewer's self-image. Don't get me wrong. He was a great guy: smart and sincere, one very dedicated to community service. He could make things happen. What I underestimated was his political savvy. When it came to politics, he was dead serious! That would become a lesson learned – for later.

During the interview I was told to sit tight while he made a telephone call to an agency next door called the Child Support

Enforcement Agency (C.S.E.A.). Until the Workfare Program position could be funded, I was told of a need in the CSEA. What happened next changed my life forever. Congratulations Johnny Boy on Politics 101. Of course, I'm being facetious. This is what happened next.

"(Name omitted), I have a good candidate here with the initial 'R' behind his name," said the director over the telephone, as he performed his sitting down version of swagger, rocking in his beautifully oval office chair. Done deal! I had the job, though another going-through-the-motions interview was scheduled with the Executive Director of the CSEA. It felt like a formality. Um, remember – I said I was desperate. Oh, how I wish I had said NO! When hearing that line about my "R" initial, that should have jolted my senses. Obviously, I got the job because I was a Republican, not because of my skills and experience alone.

I truly regret not being wiser and more courageous when hearing the "R" reference. That was not a good enough reason to take the job, unless one is applying for a position as Republican National Chairman or something like that. Yes, I am being facetious again. I was a pawn. But, I was a pawn being made promises. I'm usually pretty good at reading people, but I was taken in by the man's charm. My wife was not. I should have listened to her. Another lesson learned.

The Twelve Year War

The Twelve Year War had begun. On one hand I was grateful for the gainful employment, perceived opportunity and benefits and time with my family. It was an eight to four job. There were no weekend hours and we had an hour long lunch. Sweet, right? Wrong! That's where the other hand comes in. On the other hand, the poor management, employee abuse and office politics was nearly intolerable. Had I managed my staff at the bank in such a manner, I would have been fired in a heartbeat. But – this was the government. Everything was different. It was all about money. The public trust. I can report to you now that the government is a poor custodian of the taxpayer's money. I suspect you don't need me to tell you that.

It was the 1990's. The Cold War was thawing, but the dot.com world was just heating up. And so was the so-called global warming. Suddenly, we were a country with buildings blowing up in Oklahoma City (domestic terrorism). We had the first World Trade Center explosion (foreign terrorism). Pop culture had degraded the role of a family man. Men – fathers – were portrayed as being stupid, dimwitted, cheats and losers. I grew up with the affirmative action movement. I understood and agreed with its premises.

Women and other minorities deserved to get parity and equal rights. Like anything, however, there can be a tipping point, where the momentum of a cause becomes over-corrected or mismanaged. I know I am stepping on some toes, especially since – at times – I actually humorously enjoyed select episodes from some of the actors and celebrities I am about to criticize. But, the Roseann Barr's of the pop/shock culture age insulted me. The writers portrayed every man to look and think like an idiot. It was intentional. And it was unhealthy for our viewing public to see families portrayed as so dysfunctional. Same was true of Reba McEntire. She has a beautiful voice and many wonderful songs, but too many songs and performances about cheating, good-for-nothing men. Romantic roles were spoofed and scarred for life.

The 90's had become an era of no social conscience. Unborn innocents had no voice for their dying, aborted lives. The president of our nation uses poor discretion with an intern, giving new meaning to the word "is" (what is is). Our commander-in-chief would lie to a grand jury and get away with what we ordinary citizens would be prosecuted. Go figure. Accountability had become a national joke.

How apropos that the gigantic box office hit at the movie theaters would be Titanic! Thankfully, Disney Studios would create a form of renaissance by steering us to sanity with movies like *The Lion King* and The *Beauty and the Beast*. Lighten up folks. Just saying.... When did government, if not our nation, become such a joke? (Rhetorical question)

My life and career path was on the deck of the Titanic! My career was about to drown from the forces of politics, which as at its best or worse – depending on your moral code and political point of view. When working for the government I was enlightened on how government is not as altruistic as we are led to believe by boasting, bargaining politicians. The "collections" had more to do with government job preservation and politician's bragging rights. When young, I thought politics was an honorable profession. Older and experienced, I found politics in Central Ohio to be corrupt. Like my wife warned me – I was naïve.

Martin Yan, former editor of the Mansfield News Journal wrote extensively about Central Ohio corruption in his book, *Rotten to the Core*. He appeared on numerous nationally known television shows, such as Geraldo, CNN's Sonia Live and The Montel Williams Show. Amusingly, Mansfield, Ohio is known as the hometown of Johnny Appleseed (actually John Chapman), a legendary pioneer who planted apple trees throughout the Midwest, thus "rotten to the core." The author dedicated his book "for the people of Mansfield, who deserve[d] the very best." I wish I had known him or of his book, when working for the Central Ohio County government office during the 1990's. "I" deserved better! My family deserved better! If not for God's grace, the Twelve Year War I was embroiled in with my job might have destroyed me.

Battle lines were drawn.

The first two weeks on the job made me realize: What the hell had I done? The Executive Director had told me that he had a very serious management dilemma. I was surreptitiously and confidentially told of a problem with one of the supervisors. In code, the obvious suggestion was that I had been recruited to replace him. I guarantee you that the politicians (so well reputed for their habit of "plausible deniability" – made famous by former President Richard Nixon) who told me would deny my claim. That is what sleazy politicians do. If I had to do it over again, I would not have taken that position without a written contract or similar letter of intent. I cannot tell you how many times I was told, "Trust me." Lord, I was naïve. I swallowed the bait time and time again, having been in numerous meetings where superiors would patronize and fraternize me for advice. Looking back, how pathetic they were. The games people play.

As is common in government agencies, "deputy directors" are represented often by the opposing political party in power. One might consider such position too often as token appointments. The deputy director at the CSEA knew of my party affiliation. Publicly that individual would obviously spin it differently, but privately I can promise you she had a disdain for me from the first day of my hiring. Over the next two years the disdain would grow into animosity. She totally rejected my experience. Yet, she was savvy, using her finesse and lip service to frequently try to win me over to her point of view.

Just as I wanted to gain the confidence and acceptance of my foster father, I sought her approval. I wanted to earn her respect. Like my foster father, I never got it. After all, I was hired to replace her "guy," which later I learned - because of loose lips. There was an "understanding" with a former judge (aka God in county governance). The problem supervisor had a "protected" position. In other words, euphemism for politics. The director and deputy director had a love – hate relationship. They were good soldiers, marching to the beat that the county commissioners demanded. The ends always justified the means. Financial reports coming out of the agency and publicized by the commissioner's office monthly and quarterly were all about public relations. Or votes. No matter what – child support collections had to exceed the previous month or quarter every time! The ends always justified the means.

The supervisor I was hired to replace hated my guts. I represented everything that was wrong with politics. To be honest, he had a right to resent my hire. One day he would tell me how empathetic and admiringly he could be for both the deputy and the deputy director. He meant it. My own empathy for his personal and work history conflicted my soul. I had little regard for his management experience, virtually nothing compared to my own. He knew of my "need" for the job, seeing me as one who failed elsewhere (a fall from grace). I was a loser in his mind. How lucky he must have thought I was to get a second chance.

Practically every week he would lecture me on how I must "prove myself every single day." Like I said, my experience meant nothing to him. Nor did it mean anything to the deputy director. The director would fill my head with constant reminders to be "patient and trusting." Meanwhile, the supervisor, two weeks into my job, came out of a chair, fist clenched – ready to punch me for not giving him the answers he wanted regarding a client paying child support. The questions were interrogative in form, something I learned to do because of my background in sales and my management responsibilities. My supervisor obviously picked up on his style from seeing a few court hearings and the manner in which lawyers ask questions (from his past experience with the juvenile court judge). Except I was not on trial.

An obligor – one who makes payment for child support – came to our payment window. Typical of many disenchanted fathers, he was angry and complaining while making his payment. That can be a distraction for any cashier. In this case, it may or may not have been what is known as a flim-flam tactic. That is: One who takes a clerk into their confidence with mindless chatter. Their intention is to swindle the clerk. The cash settlement drawer was off by twenty dollars. The insinuation was clearly that "I" pocketed the money! He was trying to break me down. Naturally, my take on it was an attack on my character. It was over the top and too damn personal. Later, to his credit, he apologized.

As the years went on, I would come more into his confidence. I swear, politicians strike me as sociopaths. Ha. Over the years, while having this twelve year war, the supervisor, deputy director and director would all tell me their problems. They would supposedly confide in me their frustrations with other politicos and tell me their frustrations with the machinations of government. The movie *Office Space* could have just as easily been a government agency, rather than a private company.

Mixing community service with work can be toxic.

As written earlier, I was enjoying the benefits of time and money and how both gave me more balance between work and home. Indeed, I had steady income to provide for my family. Moreover, I had more time with my family for school activities, church functions and recreation. Also, with time, the opportunity to serve my community presented itself. I became chairman of a committee for a school levy. A school superintendent genuinely respected an idea I had advanced to a county commissioner at a luncheon. It involved an organization known as Leadership Unlimited. I felt that all school districts should combine and direct the need for school funding, foremost, through the business community (rather than each system fending for itself).

Leadership Unlimited was the perfect vehicle to drive greater awareness and funding (pro and con), since its foundation was rooted in both the business sector and that of education. For the most part, the yearly participants were up and coming young leaders in the community, sponsored by their more seasoned peers. I liked the homogenous mix. So did the superintendent - a man named Fred.

When I was a child the superintendent was a pillar in the community. He or she might expect to be in that position long-term. A student might know of one superintendent throughout their entire school experience (from kindergarten to high school). Times changed.

A Victory March

In more recent times a superintendent might have a job expectancy of five years. Central Ohio was a so-called "blue collar" community – the working class (labor-driven, as my union boss next door would remind me). The community did not like Fred. He was an outsider. By association, they turned on me too. Work and local politics were closely woven together. Taxpayers took their anger out on the schools, saying teachers were paid too much and citing poor management by the school boards, superintendents and treasurers.

It was the one thing they had a vote on. So, supporting a bond or levy was not usually a popular issue at the time. My involvement was so unpopular at work that I would be ostracized. My volunteer work meant radio and television appearances. My voice and mug shot became targets. The rant was constantly about those overpaid teachers! My wife was a teacher. You don't want to get me started. I was a witness and participant to many after hours when she dedicated her own money and time. We even had opponents to the levies come to school parking lots to make note of the make of car a teacher owned – to emphasize their materialistic argument. Their behavior was a sad commentary on our society. Talk about class warfare.

What I did not tell you yet was that I was originally a skeptic regarding the specific funding needs of the school system on a particular election cycle. I respectfully and politely challenged the superintendent on some line items in the school budget. He actually made time to meet me for lunch, when and where he convincingly explained why and what was needed. I was very impressed by his concise argument and effort taken per my query. Soon afterwards, he confided in me how he had mishandled a controversial policy problem with a popular principal. He conceded that he should have handled the matter differently. My respect for him deepened because he stepped up and took responsibility humbly. He lived and learned and was willing to apply what he learned – in the best interest of the children and the community (at great personal expense). He had character. He would amaze me by the number of hours and evenings he would sacrifice for his family, to help other families better understand what was needed to prepare their children for citizenship and work. I would see him late in the evenings. He would be totally exhausted.

Fred taught me a lesson in effective communications that would remain with me to this day. That is: When to say "I understand." I would learn and respect the tactic for its wisdom. It did not mean   "I agree" or "I disagree." It meant just what Fred said it meant: He understood. If someone disagreed with him he did not discredit them. He listened, looking for what I was taught to find: subordinate points of agreement. It was always more important what was right, not who was right or wrong. Fred showed me leadership. I made that gentleman one of my recipients for my Annual Thanksgiving Tribute. The signature speech to my public speaking series, "Lessons Learned from the University of Life," was entitled "I Understand." Then, it would be back to work – where, incredibly, I found myself shunned by some of my more politically-oriented fellow employees. One in particular – an administrator – literally requested her desk be moved away from the office space we shared. Crazy. But, grace was revealed to me by a man called Fred.

Détente

While I might have first been deemed a threat by my supervisor, only to follow with controversy over my community volunteer work, one thing prevailed: a growing dependency on my financial reporting. I made my superior look good! Unspoken in our ways, we shelved the verbal spars, placing our tactical weapons aside for the bigger cause – showing record collections that the rather large commissioner himself could brag about during his re-election campaigns.

It took a while, but slowly my supervisor began to have less and less direct control over my daily work routine. Yet, I still reported to him on the organizational chart. Some things don't change, whether it be the private or public sectors. Realistically, I was doing an administrative job (proven by comparable job classification and duties in other counties, not to speak of my fiduciary authorization with the bank and state). Routinely, I would be summoned to the deputy director or executive director's offices, to do their bidding when it came to financial reports. Without fail, the emphasis was on pleasing one commissioner in particular – the one who "ran the show." This guy was all about spin! He also was the epitome of what many might call a "fat cat" politician. I realize how cruel that sounds. But the guy enjoyed pushing his weight around. He liked making people jump! One person that would jump for him like a circus monkey was our executive director. His political survival depended upon his jumping skills. Lord, it was pathetic to watch. The commissioner fooled a lot of people. He taught at a local community college, never seeing a camera he didn't love. I'm sorry reader, but I'm telling you like it was: The guy could bloviate. He was as pompous as they came. And he survived!

Beat the heck out of me how a small community would keep re-electing someone that obvious. If this seems a bit personal to you it is because later in the story you will learn just what I meant by politics getting ugly. Honestly, I cannot imagine myself - if ever in that role – using the media, manipulating people and misleading my employees and community as much as this official did. It is called abuse of power. Current events clearly demonstrate that such is not limited to local politics. If anything, local government is where these types find their way. And once they get in power it is hard to get them out!

So, should you presume that I am being too critical or bitter, remember what the author and former newspaper editor Martin Yant wrote in his book, *Rotten to the Core*.

The author stressed, "…people of Mansfield…deserve the very best." I was in a position to witness the author's admonition. I stand by my principles and experience.

The better I made my bosses look the dirtier I felt. It was agonizing being under-employed, being that aforementioned witness to the folly around me. Other than practices I witnessed being rotten, they also seemed unethical to me.

Firing Line! Auditors Attack

The war was on! Even if I won, I would lose. Another career crisis was in the making. And there was no easy out, given the duties of my job (which first and foremost meant honoring the public trust, the oath I had taken and obeying the Ohio Revised Code – the law).

State examiners have an important function. They ensure that the taxpayer's money is being accounted for responsibly. When I was a banker, I welcomed audits. Audit findings and recommendations made us a better organization. In my government position auditors were loathed upon!

This book is an autobiography, not an operating manual on how complex government bureaucracies can function. Therefore, I'll refrain from the temptation of sharing voluminous data to justify my claims of mismanagement and political maneuvering. To protect myself, I kept copious notes. I know beyond a shadow of a doubt that state examiners had every right to question the financial reporting from the agency. It was the beginning of the end for my employment with the county. The next several years would become a defining period for my character and my life.

Not lost in the shuffleboard of my life was the unfortunate poor health of my foster father. He was deathly ill with bladder cancer. While my history and relationship was strained with him – to say the least, I would never wish a painful illness on him. However, there was irony that he was suffering from cancer – a disease he refused to acknowledge with me or his wife.

Closer to home, my wife had the onset of a long-term acute disease that eventually would take her life. That, in itself, was enough to stress most anyone. Coping with the circus at work was more than just stressful. It challenged me ethically. I was totally uncomfortable with the administrative process incorporating my job function, that being increasing fiduciary responsibilities with multiple and conflicting reporting lines. State guidelines for job classifications and organizational structuring showed my duties ridiculously out of line with comparable roles in other counties, as previous alluded to. Of course, there was a reason for that practice: It was to keep me under the control and direction of my multiple manipulating masters.

Their doings gave me low self-esteem. No arrogance intended. It's simple. My earlier training and experience prepared me to know better. I couldn't believe I had been so foolish, to allow myself to accept a position with people making so many outrageous promises. If all this was not enough, I was being attacked personally for my volunteer work on behalf our local school system. And I had an increasing role at church, which – naturally – had conflict as well. Go figure. Vocationally, socially, financially and personally my life was in chaos. The pressure was becoming almost too much to bear.

Thank God for my faith, family and close friends from church (especially Joe and Nelson and their families). They, like my wife and I, were involved in our church and schools, making for many occasions when our families would have fun times together. Those fun times were a saving grace! Given how turbulent the 90's were for me, I am sure I might have cracked under all the pressure.

Having said that, there was more to come. How much can one man take?

Thankfully, I never asked that question. I relied on faith and experience, especially that which dealt with crisis management and conflict resolution. Little did I know how instrumental that prior training would become for the war in which I found myself with the government job. And later, I would make more use of it while managing my wife's medical needs in the next millennium. It was another kind of war.

D-Day

If I let the devil take over with details, this book could fill hundreds of pages dealing with hundreds of acronyms the government is famous for, making for bureaucratic alphabet soup. Keeping it simple, let me say this: When the federal and state budgets "advance" operating funds to county governments, there must be an accounting for the disbursement and collection of public funds. If a county has a disagreement with the money advanced, there is an administrative process used to resolve the dispute. By the way, we are not talking chump change; we are talking in the millions of dollars, when accounting for a range of time, not just a static month of reporting. The county, by law, does not arbitrarily start withholding funds as they want, especially from other public entities (ie., Aid for Dependent Children or Foster Care Services).

It was almost comical, how my numerous superiors, each thinking I was their confidant, would bore me with their protestations (how their hands were tied…how political everything was…and so on). They would moan endlessly about "powers on high." I would hear all about the vendors who had campaign ties to the lawmakers and how they were low bidders contracted to software jobs beyond their capabilities or field of experience. I know. It showed every time I attempted to reconcile the Swiss-cheese programs poorly designed to settle accounts. A magician couldn't do better. As I said before: It was like talking to sociopaths.

To be fair and because it is my nature to look for the good in all people, most these so-called leaders had well-meaning rhetoric and good intentions. It did not mean they were not incompetent. They just believed their own deceptions. Remember: ends justified means. Their behavior, however, became intolerable for my principles and self-respect.

So, in that era of what "is is (or was)" and with corporate treasurers and bankers forgetting "generally accepted accounting principles" (GAAP), I saw around me a compromised culture, where the disciplines that made managers accountable no longer were enforced. Colloquially, it is the age of spin! Again, means justifying ends.

The politicians I worked for and the school boards I volunteered time to didn't know the difference between a cookie sheet and a balance sheet. They just made it up as they went along. I was no certified public accountant, but I knew what I knew and I knew what I did not know (thanks again to Mr. Plato). I knew a fair amount about settlements and financial control. I could interpret a balance sheet mostly with common sense and recollection of my coursework and corporate services. My superiors would discredit me. Why?

Because it did not serve their self-interest (or preservation). Simple. Back to the point: My superiors did what unscrupulous politicians do when they cannot get what they want. They deploy creative accounting. Hence, a sub-account was created and I was directed to bookkeep it. It would be called (drum roll please) the "ODHS WITHHOLDING AND RE-DISTRIBUTION DUE TO STATE ADVANCE DELAYS." Are you laughing? If you thought that academics are the only ones to come up with long descriptive titles for coursework, you haven't seen anything till you experience what politicians can cook up. Only problem: It was not a laughing matter. Suffice to say there was a difference of opinion between my superiors and state examiners on how advanced money is accounted for between those that disburse, report, collect and reimburse. In short, I felt strongly that we needed to be in compliance with the Ohio Revised Code!

Since I had fiduciary responsibility, signing off on state mandated reports, as well as duties associated with bank reconciliations (that was key) and other reporting, I felt liable. And I was damned if I was going to be a scapegoat for a bunch of incompetent, self-serving politicians masquerading as managers.

For the most part, the general public is indifferent to these kind of details in the administration of the public trust. And I understand that. In general, we should assume that public servants are honorable and trustworthy. You can stop laughing now. Like I said, I was naïve. I'm sure I am not alone. Who was ever going to understand the intricate details of "floating variances" and "parameter balancing" unique to the nature of my tasks? Indeed, this was one job in my life that truly was "Mission Impossible." It was a nightmare! D-Day was inevitable. And I was doomed.

My work performance is public record. I had numerous letters citing excellence in my field for spread sheeting, bank reconciliations and financial reporting. When "others of authority" took liberties with records from my office cubicle, suddenly problems developed – like records missing. How convenient. I was blindsided, if not set-up. No longer was I naïve. I choose to not cite the exact parties involved or the nature of what was "missing." It is a moot point now. And the lack of security makes it hard to prove. I'm just telling my story. For years I kept copies of all the internal memos and directives regarding how to comply (or not) with state guidelines. Had I ever asked my subordinates to do what was asked of me in the private sector I assure you I would have been fired!

My reward for doing my job too well (excellently) was having my position "eliminated." What a joke! I will tell you that no less than three local attorneys researched past comparable case histories. Each, independently came to the same conclusion: I would win a lawsuit – IF I could endure both the administrative and appellate process of the law (which could take up to several years!). In retrospect, if I had to do it over again, I would have sought an advocate from out of the county.

Either way, I could not afford such justice. That's life! For the record, on February 28, 2001, *The News Journal* (regional newspaper) had a banner heading: "County disputes findings in audit (Ohio seeks $1.4M from Richland child support enforcers.)" That was just a slice of what was a bigger pie being disputed for more than a decade. Eventually – after I was long gone – I learned of several early retirements (aka "Golden Parachutes"). I was never given that option. On July 10, 2000 I responded to a "Separation Agreement," which I reluctantly signed – eerily like the occasion my foster father forced me to sign what I believed was insurance papers for our children. My arm was being twisted metaphorically. They knew I would not put my wife through the muckraking.

The "R" behind my name was about to mean REJECTION.

With a policeman next to me (who gave me an approving nod) and an attorney sitting with me, I sat before my accusers as they ganged up on me en masse. They put on a show! The deputy director scowled at me, as she impugned my character and honesty. I swear, I could imagine her practicing her game face in the mirror the night before. The director sat on his behind, looking befuddled, yet putting up the worse acting performance ever. He totally threw me under the bus – head first! Oh, how I wish I had recordings of his "confidences" shared with me in the privacy of his office. I can forgive (as President Kennedy said), but I will never forget the man's lack of spine. For sure, my wife had him pegged. All style, no substance. Friends, I am not trying to be mean. And I refuse to play the victim role. But I paid a price for doing the right thing! Never in my life did I ever treat anyone with the indignation shown to me and my family. My language could be stronger, but this book is about grace.

Those people hurt me. More importantly, they hurt my family. I had a son in college. My wife was struggling with a long-term health problem that would eventually take her life. My former employers would not even grant me severance pay or help me find other work. The other commissioners were indifferent, one about to go to jail. Incredibly he was convicted of child molestation. You can't make this stuff up! God knows where my records were, that once upon a time were in that commissioner's custody. My immediate supervisor looked sad. For all our differences, he knew I was getting screwed (because I would not play the game – like he did).

Their accusations were baseless and without merit. But, they got what they wanted: I was out of their way! I smiled years later when learning the agency was ultimately held accountable, though it was done by political expediency. Like a friend told me, if I didn't have bad luck, I wouldn't have any luck at all. I didn't really believe in such silliness, but it felt that way.

I would go to church, only to have parishioners wonder what I did wrong. Most would say nothing. Some would ask. I was in a key leadership role with the church, so it was awkward. It was challenging to deflect the paranoia finding its way into my psyche. When alone with my thoughts and prayers, I would remember a favorite quote from John Wooden, the legendary UCLA basketball coach, who wrote, "Reputation is what other people might think you are, character is who you really are." Friends at church, such as Joe and Nelson, mentioned earlier, were of tremendous moral support to me during one of the most difficult times of my career. No one likes to have their character assaulted or reputation besmirched.

I was disgraced. And I was out of a job.

Eventually, it cost me my home and car – practically everything I owned! We were forced to declare bankruptcy. For a former banker, that meant more disgrace.

But I was wrong! God was preparing my way. Years later, as a life and career coach, I could look someone in the eye and legitimately ask, "Would you be willing to give up everything you worked for all your life to do the right thing?" Telling someone "I understand" had more authenticity to it. I had credential because I lived through the experiences of injustice. And I was a better man for it!

Lessons learned in The University of Life were plentiful during my tenure in the public sector. British historian, Lord Acton, was right when he said, "All power tends to corrupt; absolute power corrupts absolutely."

Mark Twain, humorist, gave me a reason to laugh again when feeling so hurt. Long ago he wrote, "I am quite sure now that often, very often, in matters concerning religion and politics a man's reasoning powers are not above the monkeys."

One more quote, showing nothing has changed in our American lexicon, the great humorist (a hero of mine), Will Rogers, quipped, "Everything is changing. People are taking their comedians seriously and the politicians as a joke."

Chapter (case) closed!

WORLD OF WORK: KLEINMARK, L.L.C.

It was 2003 and I was well underway with my book, *Your Pathway (to Personal Enrichment & Vocational Enlightenment)*.

The space ship Columbia, STS – 107 flew its final mission, sadly disintegrating on reentry. Homeland Security became a reality in our terrorized world. And President George W. Bush announced the capture of Saddam Hussein.

My publishing a book, seeing my copyrighted book registered in the Library of Congress was nothing compared to the aforementioned events, but for me – it was a lifetime achievement. Helping others help themselves is a passion of mine and the book has been an excellent instrument to further that mission.

Having no formal training in software, it took weeks for me to guide my way through the maze of data advertising "Web Designs Made Easy." Formatting the book was a challenge, as each page had a purpose, featuring graphics, focal points and various font sizes. It did not take me long to realize there was a learning curve for publishing and graphic design. Still, I plugged away, night and day, one page at a time, often one sentence at a time. Slowly, the text took shape. It's enlightening to realize how complex it can be to make something look and read simple. It was tedious work, but the effort was worth the patience and toil. I felt like I had a product. Most rewarding is the realization more than a decade later that the product works!

It was a strange time for my personal and professional life. Connie was still married to teaching as she was to me. I had no complaints, as I knew from the first time we met that teaching was her calling (reinforced when seeing her in her element: the classroom). Truly, she was a professional! She was a hard-working mother, devoted to her students and to her family. We always managed to take adventurous vacations with our children. We alternated cross-country visits with in-laws from Oregon every other year. Even during the difficult years when a career crisis cramped our style, we managed to make our livelihoods creative. My foster parents had both passed on and the step-monster grabbed the entire estate, as we expected would be the case. Connie and I moved on with our lives, without interference or outside criticism. But – for sure, it was a strange time because we had an empty nest. Both our boys graduated and were on their own, except for a couple brief "coming home" excursions while they were finding their place in the world.

Connie had surgery in 1994. Though the kind of operation was common for many women, it did not take long to realize that she would have protracted problems. She coped as well as expected for several years. In 2003 we agreed privately between us (with no commentaries to family or friends) that I would stay home and help with home chores, yard work and cooking. Thank God we enjoyed dining out. Ha! My cooking skills did improve over time. I follow directions well when I must (HEAT ON HIGH 15 minutes). Seriously, I had to get better in order to more effectively deal with the growing signs of fatigue and other complications associated with diabetes. No more detail, at the moment, is needed, as I am one to still honor my wife's privacy. So private was she that often details of her increasing health problems were kept from me – her own husband.

Connie had seen a lady doctor at the local hospital. Her diagnosis was later found to be incomplete. Had that doctor performed surgery – as she had planned per her diagnosis – the surgery would have been a disaster! In 2005 – through another specialist in Columbus, Ohio – Connie needed the controversial "mesh" treatment due to issues with what the medical profession calls the "pelvic floor." Without too much intrusion of Con's dignity, simply said – she had "multiple organs prolapsing."

Her internal organs were literally strangulating one another. Neither her, nor her Columbus specialist - revealed this to me! I learned about it later from the doctor during surgery, for what I was led to believe was a small tumor being removed. It ended up being the weight of a gallon of milk! And it was large! I was shocked!

Suddenly, I was coming to the realization that my wife was going to have what some might call the slippery slope. Connie recovered well, given the circumstances. She was a fighter! I continued my quest as a "life and career coach," both of us making the best – quite privately – with a situation that was growing worse. No one outside our home would know it. She would hide her pain, even from me – one who slept with her. Somehow our dog, Caddie, would sense something I could not. That dog, I swear, knew.

As the storm gathered…as Connie masked her pain…as I worked on my business, a local newspaper wrote a very nice story on January 15, 2006, featuring my book and business in their Lifestyle section. The writer quoted me as saying "I am an encourager!" Hold that thought. A few years earlier our Sunday school class studied the "I Am's" from the Book of John. In 2006, at the age of fifty-six, I felt like I knew where God wanted me to "belong." No longer would I be typecast for the man from my past. I had evolved into a purpose-driven life – one of encouragement.

I had earned it! Indeed, I did belong. God prepared me well for the role. It was humbling and pleasing to be known as an author (albeit small volume), speaker and coach. The unsolicited newspaper article redefined my image! It was grace in action.

The newspaper story printed my comments about "life being a contact sport, that sooner or later – if principled – you [we] are going to take a hit…" (And I had taken a few tough hits during my life). Little did I know more were to come! Not just to me, but especially for Connie. What we liked most about the article was what my wife said about me: That I looked for the best in everybody! That really is true about me.

Another highlight in the story was some of the quotes taken from the "Dedication" page of my book. To follow is a brief excerpt, written several days after the terrorist attack on New York City, forever known as 9/11.

"Soon after 9/11, high above the skyline of NYC, I sat on a stone wall along the New Jersey shoreline, gazing at the absence across the water. The non-existence in the distance created a stark contrast to the serene park setting around me. A multitude of mourners, like me, were writing sentiments to post on a public memorial. Soon afterward, I stood at ground zero. I thought to myself: If someone was having a bad day, they should be standing on this spot. How could anything compare?"

You see, I knew whatever I went through, it was time to stop looking back...that I had to finish a book about encouraging people in their jobs and their daily lives. The epiphany at that moment – [for which], it's not enough to live and learn. We must go one more step! We must apply what we learn. I was learning a lot! I was learning about people and more about life than what I had imagined.

Connie was holding her own. She and I had a routine. In 2007, Greg, a dear friend of mine, whom I coached, encouraged me to set new goals, specifically a triathlon! Given some of my health challenges, knee surgeries and other distractions, the idea – at first – seemed absurd. By the grace of God, however, I had several other friends, too (especially two guys named Wit and Nathan) at our local health club ready and willing to help me help myself. Ha. I had several months of conditioning to fulfill a goal and make a point – to myself. When it came time for the main event – to compete – little did I know another writer, Jon Spencer (also a member of the health club) from the News Journal, would find my personal story worthy of a featured article.

My identity in the community had changed in a matter of a few years. I was humbled when the writer inserted my "Relay for Life" speech given to Morrow County the previous summer. Mr. Spencer added "Words To Live Better By." I was sincerely flattered. I was also encouraged – in my own right – that my life had finally moved on to a better place and purpose. Below is my speech, which I fondly call my "Gettysburg Address" (because I literally wrote it on the back of an envelope in about two minutes...though, unlike President Lincoln, who was on a train). Many of the phrases I wrote from memory, having read countless books on the subject at hand. Somehow, I knitted them together for what I hoped would be an inspirational message for the rather large audience of people so directly or indirectly impacted by cancer.

Relay for Life

Hello, my name is John Klein. The name of my childhood cancer, I am told, was osteogenic sarcoma. We all have a story, don't we? A quick Google search will tell you all you need to know about that disease...and the two to five percent that survive. Getting to know me takes more effort. Cancer does not speak for me. That is my choice.

For some, cancer is like out-racing a distant cloud that finally descends upon us, engulfing us by its mystery. For others, cancer is like a pack of hungry wolves, chasing a tiring prey.

Only those who have had cancer truly know its pain – pain that lingers from the past or its teeth that bite into our present. A Japanese poet once wrote, 'We must sometimes embrace the pain to fuel the journey.'

I am here to encourage you to overcome the pain and go beyond fear, because our willpower and the grace of God are a greater ideology than any cancer cell!

Tonight, the word "relay" has relevance. When we survive a life-threatening disease we are faced with a new challenge: Surviving life!

It is good to survive. It is great to be alive!

Rather than looking over our shoulder for a closing cloud or being anxious about a stalking wolf, embrace this moment and each other with faith, hope and love.

Eventually, Heaven and Earth claims us all, whether our calling card comes in the name of cancer or not. Ultimately, our success is measured not just by how we survived cancer, but how and what we committed ourselves to in life.

Another poet described our eyes as a window into our souls.

So I ask you now, won't you take a moment to look into the eyes of those around you? What do you see? I see the love of life! Relay this love to a lonely soul and a needy world. Relay the love and the positive energy that goes with it.

Little would I know that two years later this message would speak directly to my wife. Connie and I were on the brink of a new crisis. This crisis would become very personal, not so much a career crisis, per se. Although, it would eventually end Connie's career and redirect my own. An angry cancer was invading her colon, complicated by diabetes and the multiple organ prolapsing strangling her internal organs. Incredibly, because of God's grace, what comes next also becomes an opportunity for us to witness our faith and make the last years of our marriage the most memorable, if not meaningful.

Lesson learned was how important every day is in our lives. Author John C. Maxwell published a book in 2008 entitled, *Make Today Count,* from which I modified a slogan in 2009 as a theme for the journey Connie and I were about to embark. We would call it "Staying in the Moment!" It became the fuel, resulting from pain, that inspired hundreds, if not thousands in relayed "Updates" we circulated to family, extended work family from Connie's elementary school (second largest in the state) and friends. The update was somewhat similar to *Tuesdays with Morrie*, chronicled by Mitch Albom about his regular visits with his dying professor.

In 2009 the storm no longer gathered. It struck with a vengeance!

CONNIE AND CANCER

For a few years, as indicated earlier, Connie had been coping with her 2005 surgical procedures and treatment plan. I would have my usual seasonal struggles with respiratory infections. The blusterous humid and warm temperatures becoming drizzly cold weather the next day, I swore, was going to kill me. It seemed like flu season was year-round. Every time I would get well, a setback would follow. A common cold would inevitably digress into acute bronchitis.

Then, in 2007, the central Ohio area was besieged by what would become known as the "One Hundred Year Storm." Our area was declared a disaster area. Our insurance was inadequate for the enormous property damage caused by the torrential rains and extreme flooding. FEMA (Federal Emergency Management Agency) was not useful to us due to the type of business I ran from my home. Bureaucracies! Our rental home had nearly four feet of raw sewage stagnating in our basement! Our basement we joked was our "warehouse," where we stored most our wedding gifts, nearly my entire library (sacred to me) and many other home belongings pending Connie's retirement and our impending move to Arizona. We had a five-year plan, commensurate with the capping off of a thirty year teaching career for Connie.

Only a small portion of my books, plus a few plaques and pictures were salvageable. In a word, it was disgusting. Like a fool, I attempted to clean many of the items myself, hauling nearly two tons of debris to a large trash receptacle temporarily placed in our driveway. Sure enough, it caused infections that took nearly four months to treat. And, to add to my misery, my gall bladder needed removed. Few have complications with this procedure. You guessed it! I was among the few. Ha. It was manageable, but very unpleasant. That's life! Some things didn't change. My wife kept saying again and again, "if you didn't have bad luck, you'd have no luck at all." I loved her, but it was getting old hearing that refrain. Good thing we could eventually laugh about luck, both good and bad.

As I recovered, it was increasingly apparent to me that Connie was showing more fatigue. Her appetite was not the same, as I would notice her pushing food around the plate as a young child might do. In 2008 I persuaded her to see our family doctor. She was given test strips that we all become familiar with after the age of fifty (to see if further test might be needed). She told me she took care of it; yet, I couldn't help but be suspicious. When we live with someone for more than thirty years, we tend to get to know each other pretty well. When discovering the test strips unopened in the bottom of a vanity drawer, we had a most uncomfortable discussion. She had put the test off, wishing for the best, fearing the worst. Unfortunately, the worst was to be. That choice proved to be fatal. Naturally, procrastination and fear tempt many of us to avoid some of the unpleasant tests that doctors ask of us. But, there are some things we should not ignore.

In 2009, when seeing dramatic changes in Connie's weight, disposition and general health, I took her to our family doctor against her will. He ordered a colonoscopy. It was performed on New Year's Eve, December 31st. I am not a negative person, but while in the waiting room, I had a bad feeling about what they might find. My fears were confirmed. The doctor came out, taking me to a private room and draping his arm over my shoulder. He looked me squarely in the eye and sincerely told me "how terribly sorry he was." The news was bad. Connie had advanced cancer!

Incredibly, Connie and I went to dinner at a local buffet with Dutch themes. She loved the food and the gift shop. Together, we picked out a "Hope Candle" that would be lit every night for the rest of her life. We ordered easy to digest food and talked about our future in candid terms. Simply put, she was brave. Yet, she said she would not take any chemotherapy. Many cancer patients say that at first. She changed her mind. Without the chemotherapy and radiation I was told by three doctors who work as a team that she would not live more than two or three months.

"Iron" Hach's words came to us: *John, when you have no alternative, you have no problem.* Connie had no living alternative. She chose wisely, as the chemotherapy and radiation extended her life. As it turned out over the next couple years, that decision would have some good rewards; yet, it would also yield some bad moments and difficult memories, as I will explain later in this chapter.

Connie was scheduled for surgery. Our hope was that the tumors could be removed and treated, allowing her to teach another year and enjoy years of retirement in Arizona with our two children. What else could possibly go wrong? Sigh. With less than three weeks before her scheduled surgery, our town experienced a blizzard. The question I just posed was answered by her slipping on ice that formed on our patio. Connie was retrieving our pet dog, Caddie, out of the deep snow. When she fell, she broke her primary wrist, causing a compound fracture! It required immediate surgery. While being treated initially at the Urgent Care facility, her heart rate dropped suddenly, causing her to be rushed by ambulance – through a blizzard – to the hospital. It was critical mass. One thing kept leading to another thing. And none of it was good.

The orthopedic surgeon performed the needed surgery on her wrist successfully; however, three to four months of physical therapy would be needed – after her colon surgery. I teased her about the contraption with pins piercing her wrist. They had screw heads on them that the doctor would adjust on follow-up appointments. It was needed to hold her bones together and set hand and wrist in the desired position for healing. When I would be near her I would tell her my cell phone reception improved. It would make her laugh. And I decided right then and there that I would make her laugh at least once a day for the rest of her life. I came within six days of that goal (the last six days being spent at a Hospice facility in Phoenix, where she no longer had the strength to move or express herself).

Late in January of 2009 Connie was in the operating room. The outcome would make it one of the worse days of my life. Connie's dear teaching friend, Karyl, a caring lady from our church and our minister, Pastor Chris were with me in the waiting room. To be honest, I wanted to be alone; but, discretion was in order over valor, as they loved Connie too. They wanted to support and comfort me, almost as if they knew the foreboding news the doctor would tell me later.

The surgeon was a man with an outstanding reputation, not just for his competency, but for his compassion. Several hours into surgery he called me into a private room. In layman's terms he calmly, yet with a measured sense of urgency, asked my permission to perform an "end-sigmoid colostomy with recto-sigmoid resection with what the medical profession calls a Hartmann's pouch." Candidly, he further explained the additional complications not previously evident from tests involving her earlier mesh replacement. Scarring and adhesions were more extensive than previously known. He said the tumors were "angry" (meaning very aggressive). I had to make a choice – for my wife. It was either the aforementioned procedure (which the doctor had done before) or my giving him permission to be adventurous, which likely would fail and possibly cause Connie more harm.

It was like a kick in the solar plexus. I literally made an involuntary guttural sound, knowing it was a seminal moment, one where her life, that which was left to her, would radically change the quality and outlook of her life! Would she ever forgive me? Would I be able to take care of her? Of course, the decision was a no-brainer. There was only one "right thing" to do. Common sense (at least for a doctor) suggested the decision was quite academic. He knew what he needed to do, as did I.

A lesson learned from this sad day was that of not being too proud to know when we need support, no matter how strong we think of ourselves. Also, those we love are loved by others too. I am glad friends were there for her and me, as I would not have gotten through that gut-wrenching day without their comfort and support. Not lost from the experience is our utter dependence on God. Thank God, prayer is a first resort, not last. In truth and intuition, I was more ready to make a difficult decision during a crisis than I gave myself credit for most my life. God is light years ahead of us.

As much as I would like to take credit for it, fact is God prepared me well for the role of being a caregiver, just as He prepared me for every role in my life. Amazing Grace is a song that speaks to me in life, not just funerals. I am truly amazed at how God prepares our way. When I look at my life now as a life and career coach, it was God's "gentle nudges" – far more than my own direction – that led me to my calling. There is something to be said about obedience. Wise choices are dependent on doing God's Will, not our own.

My caregiver role began the day after Connie's surgery. Incredibly, I was the one to first tell her of her fate. Daringly and against hospital regulations, I carefully and gingerly climbed into Connie's hospital bed, competing with impersonal paraphernalia sustaining the patient's needs. I snuggled up to her, indifferent to her colostomy encumbrances, softly whispering in her ear the message inscribed on the timepiece I had given her on our wedding day: "Today I love you more than yesterday." Two unspoken rhetorical questions were answered: One, there was no need for "forgiveness," as she trusted me and knew we would adapt and commit to whatever was needed to extend her life. Two, my strength came from God, reinforced by the support of others that prayed for us. We were never truly alone. We were stronger than we knew.

CONNIE'S VICTORY MARCH

Victory is defined as a success or triumph over an enemy. The title of this book may be a narrative of my own triumphs, but my wife was nothing less than courageous in her own victory march with cancer. It always bothers me a bit when it is written that "cancer claimed" someone. We belong to a loving God – not some Cancer God. We have no promises that pain and suffering won't inflict our being. We do have a promise from On High, as written in the Book of Life, Romans 8:37-39:

"No, despite all these things, overwhelming victory is ours though Christ, who loved us. And I am convinced that nothing can ever separate us from God's love. Neither death nor life, neither angels nor demons, neither our fears for today nor our worries about tomorrow – not even the powers of hell can separate us from God's love. No power in the sky above or in the earth below – indeed, nothing in all creation will ever be able to separate us from the love of God that is revealed in Christ Jesus our Lord."

Connie's victory march began the moment she was conscious of my policy-breaking presence, when snuggling with her in the hospital bed. When leaning into her I declared, "You are going to fall in love with this [ostomy] bag!" True to our faith, it was not a debate; it was a decision. As Iron Hach would have reminded us: There was no alternative. Therefore, we had no problem. Instead, we had an opportunity to witness our faith. It was all about attitude and faith. While Connie slept through a medicated recovery, I meditated. All evening and through the night I sensed what was yet to come. Without complaint, I went to the hospital library and started reading about her disease. There were earlier signs, so I was not totally in the dark. But there was more to learn in order to provide her the care and comfort she deserved.

I am not going to be shy about being a prayer warrior. From what I had learned, the journey ahead was going to take inordinate energy. There would be uncertainty and numerous perils along the way. The treatment plan had been well explained to both of us, but one doctor in particular (the lead doctor of the trio of specialist) made it a point to speak directly to me regarding her care. He told me that he was acquainted with my own experience. As I listened to him, my confidence grew. Somehow I knew I would be up to the task. Rarely had I met such a caring and professional person in the medical field. During one of Connie's hospitalizations, the doctor admonished a nurse for not referring to his patient by name. He literally scolded the young lady with this explanation: "None of my patients are Room 209 – or whatever; they go by a name! Please refer to my patient by her name! My patient's name is Connie Klein! Do you understand?"

Later, when we moved to Arizona, quite honestly – that personal touch was long gone. To be fair, the doctor to patient ratio is more demanding in a major urban sprawling metropolis. But, I have to applaud the care providing team we had in Mansfield, Ohio.

Connie relented to chemotherapy (without it, she was doomed, so we were told. And soon.) She – and I – tolerated it well. Radiation was another matter. She was hammered with the maximum doses every day, except weekends. Later, a doctor would describe the effects on her digestive tract like that of "wet tissue paper." She was never able to eat normally again.

Concurrent with chemo treatments at the oncology center and the daily doses of radiation, Connie was in physical therapy three times a week for her broken wrist. When not at therapy, we had to do exercises at home. It was a grind. So, I set up a schedule, making what we had to do more a routine. Included would be fun activities, like playing Scrabble or going to the library to get Connie her favorite novels. She got hooked on game shows, which meant the Game Show Network got lots of play in our home. She particularly liked *Wheel of Fortune*.

There were times that my brain was buzzing from the inane banter of the guests. Connie would make the shows a platform of competition between us. It was healthy for her, but I did think my brain was going to explode at times. Ha. We really committed ourselves to the tasks at hand. She trusted me to her personal care needs. And I would never make her feel self-conscious with what had to be done. We were a great team! For a year or so, we could be fairly mobile – even going out to restaurants. She would sit at the table, unselfishly, and engage me in conversation while I ate my meal. Illness had changed everything, yet we behaved as if nothing had changed.

Days turned into weeks and weeks into months. After nine months the chemotherapy and radiation phase of the treatment plan came to an end. While we never gave up on hope, the austere prognosis was all too familiar to me. Research of clinical outcomes was discouraging. Connie's determination was extraordinary considering that she already exceeded some of the statistical margins. As you will read further along in this chapter, the radiation and chemo might have turned her organs into "wet tissue-like" substance, but it did not destroy the fire in her belly! Her willpower and my coaching would soon form a nexus from which her memory would make a connection with the next generation.

Our five-year plan came to fruition as we realized our dream to move to Arizona. In September of 2009, Connie having taken an earlier retirement than what she had wanted, was ready to join the children already living in the Valley of the Sun. My youngest son, having some experience with property management and knowing what kind of home we were looking for, scoped out real estate listings in the west valley. He found a three-bedroom ranch with a swimming pool and two baths. Perfect! It was a home that had been foreclosed on, which meant we would likely have a lot of "sweat equity" to put into bringing the house up to par. Given the federal housing program available at that time, our dream to once again be homeowners became our reality! I could have a den and there would be a guest bedroom available for visitors. In the months ahead, I would take Connie into the pool and perform water aquatics with her, helping her maintain some muscle tone. My son Doug sent pictures over the internet. It was a beautiful neighborhood, where many parks existed and surroundings made one feel as if they were living in a horticultural center.

Late in September I put Connie on a plane with our dog Caddie. She would stay at Doug's home for three days until I arrived with the twenty-seven foot rental truck packed wall-to-wall. Two days before departing I had a garage sale. I wrote a story about the experience, but will spare you. I have never been a fan of garage sales. I fear if sharing that satirical story I might compromise my theme of grace. My saving grace, of course, is humor. I will ask you this dear reader: Am I the only one who sticks a price tag on a garage item for a nickel, only to have some moron ask I would take a penny? Ha! I even had handicap accessibility. Believe it or not, I had a senior citizen bus stop! Half the passengers appeared to be auditioning for Tim Conway's hysterical impersonation of a shuffling old man. I sold everything! I put a sticker on my broom. My neighbor - one to get my humor – bought it! I was ready. My swimming buddy and his son helped me load the truck. We shared an early morning breakfast afterwards at Denny's. It was time to say goodbye. I was alone, heading westward.

What else could possibly go wrong?

It didn't take long for that query to be answered. The truck transmission was slipping throughout the entire trip, which caused the truck to not accelerate more than forty-five miles an hour. I could have had the rental company own up to their agreement, but I was not about to stop the truck, wait forever and a day, only to unload and load all over again. So, I kept going – like an old man in the sea with one paddle. Next, the truck started splattering oil from the exhaust. I was pulling our car on a trailer. Later, the Ford Focus would need detailed in Arizona. When crossing the borders of New Mexico and Arizona I was giddy. The long descent began on Interstate 17, from the high elevations of Flagstaff down to the valley floor of metropolitan Phoenix. My emotions had as much momentum as my descending truck wheels. As I pulled up to my new home I was singing like Clark Griswold, butchering Michael Buble's lyrics: "It's a new day…a new life…and I am feeling good."

Finally, when returning the truck – I swear I am not making this up – I had to use the emergency brake! The truck lost its brakes when returning it. To my pleasant surprise, when writing the rental company to complain, they actually refunded me most the cost for the truck.

Lesson learned was that sometimes companies actually do make good on their advertising. Though I had driven thousands and thousands of miles a few years earlier for an expediting company, I had never driven nearly non-stop for three days and nights. America is a big country!

Connie was tolerating the transitional treatment phases well, surprising all the doctors. We were referred to new doctors in the Greater Phoenix Area. We had adapted to a routine that involved her enjoying her new home and being able to take short rides to her favorite places – like the shopping mall. The next few weeks and months our kids and their friends helped paint the interior of our new home. We bought furnishings from local stores and had our beds and some appliances delivered. We were settled into our new home, meeting new neighbors and hearing from a gazillion people who wanted to visit sunny Arizona. Connie was doing well enough that I was able to join a health club nearby, which was her idea.

Life is good, right? Retired and living a new life in the Valley of the Sun, were we! While not really called remission, Connie was living with her cancer, so to speak. She was upbeat and looking forward to an extended life with the children. The nexus I spoke of earlier (Connie's willpower and my coaching) had to do with the notion of Connie living long enough to see her first grandchild. I'll elaborate on that matter later in this chapter. Meanwhile, there was a setback.

Heart Attack

On December 18, 2009 at 6:30 p.m. – at the health club – I had a heart attack in front of locker number 141. By the grace of God the only person in the locker room at the time, other than myself, just happened to be the son of a doctor. As first responder he knew exactly what to do. The other point of grace was my being a few miles from what is reputed as one of the best heart hospitals in the state! I work at being healthy, so the event caught me completely by surprise. I had trained for and performed in 5/K running events and performed in a triathlon. My dietary habits were good and my workouts were regular.

When I think of some of the walruses I've seen vegetating in the sauna at the health club, life simply seems unfair. It seems like they should be the ones having a heart attack! As I found out later, my situation was mostly due to genetics, though I wouldn't know much about it due to being raised in a foster home. The doctor told me I had "crooked arteries." Coronary artery disease was the farthest thing from my mind. The good doctor placed three stents in my heart. Like Connie, I would be joining her in convalescence. For the next several months I would do cardio rehab, together with taking dietary classes.

Before being taken by ambulance to the hospital, gym staff had taken emergency contact information from my wallet, thus calling my son. Soon, both sons, daughter-in-law and wife would be at the hospital as quick as the ambulance. When my youngest son was standing next to the stretcher, I vaguely recall telling him, "Be sure to tell the rest of the family how much I loved them." Note the past tense. I actually did not think I would survive! There is a myth about having a heart attack.

Many think it is a great way to go, so to speak…to die. Fast, right? Not necessarily so. Other than having a feeling of nausea and weakness – it is actually very exhausting. I wanted so bad to place my head down and close my eyes. The first responder, then paramedics kept my head in the game.

My point is this: I was ready if God had chosen that moment to bring me home to Him. I take some comfort and peace of mind with knowing that I was "ready" – first in my childhood, then again in my adult life to meet Jesus. My heart and mind were in good places.

While progressing through cardio-rehab, knowing I had dodged a life-threatening bullet, Connie and I were more determined than ever to weather the storms of life. Three months later I would find myself taking walks: Three hundred feet at a time. While my recovery was slow, Connie seemed to have an extra bounce in her step. Her stamina had improved. Her diet had not. She was already very limited, mostly to a liquid diet, and it was a matter of time before she would experience a relapse. A questionable colonoscopy was the culprit. I was unhappy with the procedure performed by an inexperienced doctor. Following the procedure Connie immediately experienced multiple complications and blockages that would put her back in the hospital for several days on more than one occasion. What ensued was multiple infections, blood disease and a recurrence of her cancer – more angry than ever before.

Catastrophic Cancer

My wife was adamant about not being cared for in a nursing home. Her condition, sadly, had worsened, becoming catastrophic. It was if every system in her body was under assault! I use that extreme word because her treatment was now as life-threatening as the disease itself. Her diabetic condition, along with the infections, the metastasizing cancer and nutritional challenges were a nightmare. Every action had a reaction. One thing led to another: Critical mass! The learning curve for her caregiving got steep, making me feel like I was studying to become a nurse.

Connie's primary doctor would not underwrite or authorize an intravenous treatment plan using TPN's (Total Parenteral Nutrition) if administered from our home. We were told that Connie's medical "markers" (age, diabetic, advanced cancer, etc.) could expect a TPN plan to extend her life, perhaps two or three months. The doctors did not know Connie. Whether they knew the Lord or not would be another question. I had ONE DAY to find Connie a doctor, otherwise our hand was forced to use an emergency room, whereupon a nursing home would be next. Once again, God's grace prevailed! A pharmaceutical provider gave us a lead (incredibly kind people).

A young doctor, part of a larger group in Downtown Phoenix agreed to see her. He took on the challenge. When seeing him the next day, he was immediately convinced that Connie and I had the "right stuff" to manage her care at home. He was willing to prescribe the needed TPN's, open-ended! It was our only hope for any kind of extended quality of life. The doctor turned to me, saying, "You're the life coach. So, coach – we need a goal! What say you?"

I looked at Connie and boldly said to her and the doctor, "Our daughter-in-law and son are expecting our first grandchild in six months. Our motto will be 'STAY IN THE MOMENT.'"

Connie loved it! The doctor, young and personable, liked it too. It was a strange moment. Here we were: Connie, her new specialist (one of nine doctors in the past year) and myself – all excited about adding a few more months of life for my wife, so that maybe she might welcome our grandchild into this world, knowing she would soon be leaving it.

There was something priceless and timeless about a "precious moment," one that our future grandchild would look back on one day and marvel at the pictures capturing such a memory.

The months ahead became challenging. I had to do things differently due to the increasing physical demands. My right arm limited me as did exertion issues associated with my heart. Connie and I did not despair. Connie enjoyed the MacGyver television series, which aired during the 1980's and '90's, featuring Angus MacGyver, special secret agent, who would jerry-rig paper clips, duct tape or whatever to solve problems. Like I said earlier, every day I made my wife laugh. So, setbacks became opportunities for my physical comedy. Somehow, I would MacGyver whatever needed done, invariably making Connie laugh through our pain (yes, I felt it too).

Incredibly, I would become accustomed to THREE HOUR intervals of sleep, as Connie's care required 24/7 around-the-clock attention. I would take melatonin, often used by people in the airlines industry for jet lag, or by nurses and doctors working swing shifts in hospitals. There would be multiple hospitalizations, in which I would stay with her in the hospital – still providing her personal care. As a consequence, I contracted MRSA (Methicillin Resistant Staphylococcus Aureus) – sometimes life-threatening (especially for those with compromised immune systems). This staph bacterial infection is known to be associated with healthcare facilities. It begged the question I was becoming all too familiar with: What else could possibly go wrong?

God only knows where I found the strength to manage Connie's continuing care. What doctors originally predicted would be a two or three month extended life span became EIGHTEEN MONTHS! Not only did Connie's victory march include the "money shot" (as my son would call it) – that of holding our granddaughter Elliot – Connie went on to live another year to enjoy that baby. She also got to say goodbye to her teaching friends and have quality time for family before the "Comfort Care" phase began. By the way, the photograph (money shot) – the precious moment – sets framed on an end table in my living room.

Good, right? Not so simple. During one of her hospitalizations, Connie acquired a severe blood infection and a high fever, basically called sepsis. Twice she was not expected to make it through the night. Miraculously, she would rally – making her feel invincible. Sometimes fate has a way of testing our convictions. Once again, I was placed in an unenviable position (not unlike the time in January of 2010, when the surgeon asked me to make a choice: Be adventurous, possibly costing Connie her life or do the irreversible procedure, extending life – but life never being the same).

Connie was breaking the fever and we were again faced with a choice. TPN's were now turning against her, which they are known to do over time. TPN's were her enemy now. She could go off the TPN's and submit herself to hospice / palliative care, which would focus on the caring, not the curing. We would be able to do this in our home, at least, to the very end (days), where more medicine and care could be administered on-call to manage her pain and symptoms. The other choice was to continue the TPN treatment plan, albeit at high risks. In actuality, it could prolong her suffering.

Connie was a stubborn one. As I mentioned, her rallying was making her feel invincible. Emboldened, she did not want to surrender to hospice. I made a calculated and faithful decision, telling my wife of over three decades that I would not interfere with the sanctity of life. After praying and thinking through it carefully, it was my strong belief that such a decision was between Connie and her Lord. I pledged to my wife that I would honor and live with whatever decision she came to with our Lord. The easier one for me would have been her immediate succession into hospice care. That was not Connie's choice. Connie, again, chose life! I will never second guess her decision. But that decision tested my faith, as I would watch her suffer for it. Again, God showed His grace. Because of grace, I was able to continue my victory march, though the road ahead would be most difficult. No one said it would be easy.

Comfort Care

Comfort care almost seems like an oxymoron. The only hospice care we had in the home was that of lab work. A home nurse by the name of Sandy would take her blood, so TPN's could be reformulated by the pharmaceutical laboratory. The lab was a godsend. So was the home nurse. They were Connie's lifeline. I read extensively about anticipatory mourning (not having forgotten the "lessons learned" from when my foster mother and father both needed care in their final days). Most noteworthy was a book by acclaimed author and journalist Gail Sheehy (Passages series), who chronicled her care-giving experience with her husband (that most her readers never knew about until after she wrote the book). The book's title was *Passages for Caregiving*. It was enormously instructive and a helpful guide.

In all honesty, until you experience such emotional, mental, financial and physical demands, nothing can fully prepare a caregiver for some of the unexpected behavior one goes through with a dying spouse (or any loved one), including several months of horror in the form of emesis (If you think looking that word up and reading it is disturbing, try coping and appreciating what nurses and caregivers do for a loved one's personal care needs every day and night in hospitals and nursing homes). Our problem was unique, at least to us: We had no nurse. Connie would absolutely have NO ONE but me for her personal care. I married her for sickness and health.

As said earlier, I kept my vow. Protecting myself was no easy task, especially when doing so with dignity. Ms. Sheehy's book reminded me that I could draw upon my management training – to be an effective and loving caregiver. That meant planning several loads of laundry around the clock, having checklist to audit all my medicating responsibilities. It meant being prepared for contingencies, such as a paramedic friend being available to give me advice, even if it was only what language to use when talking to a clinician over the phone (just the facts please). It meant ordering supplies ahead of time. It meant arranging visitations that coincided with Connie's energy levels. Like anyone who has been there, it's a LOT of work! Yet – it was a labor of love.

I was committed to Connie passing from this life to the next with the least amount of pain and the ability to say goodbye to all her family and friends on her terms (as much as possible, anyway). To be honest, some people did not make that easy. Like all families, sometimes there is divisiveness or brokenness. Our family at-large was no different. If you are looking for the juicy nature of the conflicts involved, it won't come from me.

Again, Ms. Sheehy's book was incredibly useful – even in that regard. She even helps with how to talk to doctors and deal with insurance companies. That would prove to be more saving grace after Connie passed away.

No matter how much morphine I legally gave my wife, it was not enough. In June of 2012 obvious signs of her imminent death were apparent to me. Not to Connie. For a lady who never had much threshold for pain, she endured unspeakable pain her final days. She refused to leave her home and the side of Caddie (who knew). She wanted only me and no one else to touch her. The end was near – so far as how we know it in this realm. But Connie would have no part of it! She just would not make peace with the inevitable. I struggled for many, many days over whether to include some of what I am about to write in my narrative, finally deciding to do so. It might help another along the way be prepared for similar sadness. Connie was angry – if not hateful towards me the last six days of her life. I agonized over it, yearning for the kind of closure we read about in romance books or see on made-for-television dramas or in the movies.

I was physically exhausted, totally unable to meet the demands of her "comfort care," without seeing her suffer mercilessly. In good conscience and prayerful judgment – I made that final telephone call to hospice. The time had come for my wife of thirty-six years to be transported to a facility where greater doses of morphine could be administered and TPN's discontinued. Once again I was reminded of Mr. "Iron" Hach's words, "John, when you have no alternative, you have no problem." It didn't help. For six days and nights I would be at her side, just her and myself (with the children stopping in and out, making their last goodbyes, waiting for my call). How I wanted some soft words, under a fading breath while slow rhythms of her chest barely moved up and down. Just a squeeze of her hand, which once in a while I got.

Unmistakably, was the movement of her eyes. We had a blinking code the first couple days at the Ryan House – the last house she lived in. The "eyes" had it, those being all that I would get for me to feel "comforted."

On the last night (morning actually/middle of the night), Connie's body summoned me to her side for one last embrace and gaze into her beautiful green eyes.

We stayed in the moment – a moment that will last for eternity.

From Heaven, I knew she would understand…perhaps – forgive.

Celebration of Connie's Life

It has been my commitment to honor my wife's wishes, which at times – to be honest – created conflict. Her not wanting anyone but she and myself knowing of the extent of her illness (to keep it from our children, especially) produced some strained feelings and misunderstandings. Cancer, as is said often, impacts not only the patient, but family and friends. Our sons, in retrospect, I believe should have been better informed. Information swirling around private matters, but affecting others can be tough calls.

They are relative to the dynamics of each family's intensely personal history and circumstances. Just another reason prayer should always be a first resort, not last. It is why grace is the centerpiece of all I do. For as much of it as I try to show others, I can only pray it is sometimes returned in kind. When looking back (a lesson learned), I am not going to beat myself up too much for any shortsightedness. Battling cancer on so many fronts is hard enough without piling on one's self. The key is to not make any big mistakes – especially in the personal and comfort care of a loved one (such as not knowing what to do during a diabetic episode or giving the wrong dose of medication).

We were able to witness God's love and our own through the periodic "updates," which humorously were signed off as Connie's "scribe." Often we would both or individually receive thoughtful comments or telephone messages on what our words of encouragement meant to others in their daily lives, not to mention how "staying in the moment" really did "make each day count" (thank you Mr. John C. Maxwell, for writing your books of inspiration).

There is no need to recite all that was said at the two memorials, one in Arizona (for family, especially those on the west coast) and another at our former church in Mansfield, Ohio (where most her and my own extended families, personal and work-related knew her from). It was like any other memorial service, each having their own anecdotal stories shared, each with flowers and well-wishes from caring people. In Ohio, I have some friends who run a funeral home. It amazes me how incredibly professional and sensitive they are to the wide range of situations, customs and needs of those who mourn their loved ones. Suffice to say, in each service, there were beautiful memories, music and prayers, which I'll elaborate on in a moment. First, I want to tell you about the director of the mortuary and crematory in Arizona. He could borrow some eloquence from my funeral buddy in Ohio. Let me explain the lighter side of final arrangements.

Connie's wish was to be cremated. Therefore, when making final arrangements with the mortuary and crematory, together with the cemetery, a double-sided niche was chosen for our final resting place.

The cemetery associate asked me, "John, which side would you like to be on?" My reply was, "The RIGHT," with considerable emphasis! Before the associate could ponder, I quipped, "Sir, you'd have to know my wife. For once in my life I want to be 'right.'" He laughed heartily. I did too. I knew my wife well. She undoubtedly was laughing from Heaven, saying to another angel, "Some days I don't know what to do with him."

More amusing than my joke about the niche was the experience with the good folks at the Arizona mortuary and crematory. When my wife passed away at the hospice facility, I pretty much trusted the hastily made plans made with this nearby facility. Money, on the heels of so much medical expense, can be a concern. In our case the bills had become astronomical, involving a dozen medical providers (which is a separate story unto itself). I was trying to be dignified, yet cost-conscious. Let me put it this way: When first meeting the owner, he had all the empathy and professionalism one should expect from such an experience. After I prepaid him for his services, the rest got interesting, if not – at times – strange. Each subsequent visit for planning purposes, setting up the room and getting questions answered became something out of a sitcom script. There was a large dog on the loose. The roaming

A Victory March

dog made himself comfortable anywhere he wanted to be. He acted as if he owned the place. The director morphed into Boss Hogg, the character from the old *Dukes of Hazzard* television series. He had all the props: The cigar, hat, suit and tie and belly to match. His assistant, responsible for cremation looked like Lurch (I'm not kidding) from the *Addam's Family*, another television show from the 1960's. Thank God, though mostly left to myself to find microphones, podium and assorted sundry items for a service, it all went nicely. Connie, however, would have wondered where did we find this character? Perhaps if they weren't quite up to par as others, she would also find it in her heart from Heaven to include this episode in my aforementioned supplication for forgiveness.

Point is: No one knew but my son and myself. Weeks and months following, my sons and I had a few laughs reminiscing Boss Hoggs, Lurch and the dog.

Seriously, one segment of each memorial – Arizona and Ohio – was the playing of a song I recorded weeks earlier (No way would I ever do it live, as it would have made it too much about me. Besides, trying to sing a song at your own wife's memorial service is asking a lot emotionally). You guessed it. It was, indeed, the song I sung to Connie on our wedding day on April 17, 1976 *–And I Love You So*. It is a beautiful ballad, as I've said more than once. Nothing changed over the decades. I loved her so. She loved me. Don McLean of *"America Pie"* fame wrote lyrics to one stanza we both loved: "The Book of Life is brief...but once the page is read, all but love is dead...That is my belief!"

And so it was and is. Connie still lives in my heart. And that is why author Michael Connelly's fictional character, Harry Bosch's "single-bullet theory" has so much prominence with me. He believed there can be only one lady that will pierce a heart for a lifetime. That is my belief. I do not want to compare another woman to Connie at my age.

I had one marriage and I was a one-woman man and that is how it is going to be. Now, I am married to those who remain. My mission remains also – to encourage others (which is a good segue to the final chapter of this book).

VICTORY!
MOVING ON,
MARCHING FORWARD

During the past twelve years, starting my small enterprise called Kleinmark, LLC., publishing my modest book and coaching others with their life and careers often made me what I called "someone's temporary best friend." At times, I could overwhelm someone with my testimony. And I could overwhelm myself, as I have no staff, agent or structure to filter the demands that can occasionally go with my kind of work in this kind of underemployed work environment and social culture. I am sincerely humbled by the need and the trust others have placed in me as their Encourager.

I have learned that old-fashioned word-of-mouth is still a potent form of advertising. Reputation matters. When moving to Arizona, given all the healthcare needs of my wife, little did I expect such a demand for my services. Never was I prominent, rich or famous. Always, I have been busy! And I love what I do. When I meet people and help them help themselves, indeed – it feels like we're temporary best friends.

The old Irish saying from J.A. Foley, one close to my heritage, keeps coming back to mind:

"I don't set up to be no judge of right or wrong in men, I've lost the trail sometimes myself...an may get lost again; An' when I see a chap who looks as though he'd gone astray, I want to shove my hand in his and help him find his way."

My cardiologist, several close friends and common sense told me there are limits to how emotionally involved one can become in   the helping business. As they have encouraged me, it was time to write a book, to let my book become someone's friend just as books have been my friends through the years.

From my boyhood emerged a battered soul who once trembled with fear from the sharp warnings and threatening hand of a fear-mongering foster father. Now I am a gentle soul, having forgiven a tyrant, who at one time was likely battered and indoctrinated by demons of his own. My foster father was taught to admire Adolf Hitler, which he did to his dying day. History taught me well, helping me to not only understand the country and world I was born and raised in, but preparing me to understand God Almighty. He created beauty. Man, too often, corrupts His Creation, including that of His own image. Beyond a foster father…beyond father figures – I had the Father of all fathers! Through it all, I have been saved by His grace.

As I reflect on my lifetime and the upholsterer from Pittsburgh who hammered me with his wretched ways, I am certain that he never was shown the kind of love that could make him appreciate the blessing of fatherhood. My foster father estranged his adopted son too. While trying to give him a graceful way out of his meanness, it is not lost on me that others came from such awful circumstances without becoming abusers. God reveals Himself to all, I believe – should they choose to be open to His Holy Spirit. My foster father had the tenets of the Catholic Church to guide him, yet he chose to forsake their teaching and support. That was my foster father's failing, not the church. At least my foster mom tried to be a mother. She worked hard, but she, too, was a battered soul throughout my lifetime. My foster mom knew my biological mother before I knew her, with my learning of her on my foster mother's death bed. Once again, the prevailing attitude was to forgive, innately understanding the irony of the moment, and to ask mercy on a dying soul, who – in my arms – tearfully was feeling inadequate as a mother. It was a saintly woman who would sign birthday cards to me with "Mom #3." By the grace of God, in my adult life she became the closest person to ever being a real mother to me. Connie and I called her Mom Hach.

When Connie passed away an associate at Resthaven Cemetery, where she was interred – knowing the long-term caregiving role we endured – heartened me by softly saying, "John, don't feel guilty for having a sense of relief." He was right. For several years I was trying to be Superman, not only for Connie's sake – with so many of her personal preferences and needs in strictest confidence, but for the many people pulling on my cape for life and career advice (not knowing the full extent of our personal lives). While Connie might rest in peace, I had unfinished business ahead of me for another year and a half (negotiating debt settlement with many medical groups, insurance companies and third-party collectors. It was like having a full-time job). One of Connie's former students had my back. He went on to become a lawyer in the Greater Cleveland Area. Our family watched him grow up, along with our own kids. When visiting Arizona on other business, he came by to see me, bearing documents that would prove to be useful with Arizona's laws. He gave me great advice.

Rather than have, um – excuse me – what he called a pissing contest between lawyers, he encouraged me to use my experience, especially my writing skills. In short, I went on a writing campaign with debtors, appealing to them on "humanitarian grounds." When finally achieving some "victories" (for want of a better word), I moved on, marching forward – thanks, also, to some great advice from my sons who told me I earned the planned move to a country club community. I preferred to think of it as God's way of rewarding me for taking good care of my wife. When moving into my condominium complex, suited perfectly with a writing room (or as I call it, The Hemingway Room), I stopped writing and sauntered over to the golf range where, quite literally, a prayer of mine was answered. I met a young fellow aspiring for great things in the game of golf.

As a life and career coach – an encourager – I knew I could give him positive energy, having taken notice of his work ethic and commitment to drills. Sometimes we just trust our instincts. Deep down I confess that my wanderings had the motive, if not hope that I might make a friend in golf…someone that would remind me of my old buddy Dave whom I had lost to cancer just before Connie passed. The stranger on the range genuinely extended his hand to me in friendship. Nick has been a blessing in my life. Every day I look forward to working with him…supporting him…encouraging him in his quest to elevate his game to professional standards. Likewise, he tirelessly takes time to teach me daily on the advantages of the modern golf swing.

Several months ago he told me how he believed God brought me into his life for a reason. I get a kick out of watching him analyze videos, how he illustrates the golf swing with an economy of words – not to mention watching him perfect his own swing and game. I learn from watching him and listening to his instruction. He has me doing things doctors and others said I would never be able to do. Speaking of reason – nearly a year after we met, a tragedy struck his family. I don't want to go into the details, as I want to respect the family's privacy and need for healing, but the "reason" went beyond golf. If ever I was placed in a position to give encouragement, it was for his family during their time of loss. Just "being there" in a support role gave me reason to reflect on my own losses. I meditated on how grace came my way again through the quality of relationships...the kind of friends I was making. It reminded me again about the torch being held for others, how it brightens our own way that much more.

Despite tragedies from my own past, life moved on, opportunities presented themselves – only to reveal the abiding grace, should we only realize its beauty. I had realized a dream that I never expected to see in my lifetime: To live on a golf course and have great golfing buddies, all of which was part of a lifestyle that continues to redefine...or should I say refine my life? Victory!

No longer do I feel as if I "don't belong." My family is well-provided for. My legacy is established. My conscience is clear. Thank you...no – check that: Bless you reader, for taking an interest in my story. Before we say goodbye, and my sharing some closing thoughts, allow me to recap some of my journey, picking up on the middle school years. Then I would like to leave each and every one of you with some questions to ponder in the corridors of your minds. The lessons we all live and learn in life can be applied by adopting principles to live by. They will be unique to your own experiences.

Junior High School (Middle School) swallowed me, nearly breaking my spirit. The mind of a young boy or girl can feel desperate when shunned and avoided because they are different...because they have the misfortune of being in an unloving and broken home environment. Being socially awkward and sickly-looking, while not even knowing what name to use on your school papers does not foster confidence or a strong personal identity. Yet – through it all my inferiority complex eventually was overcome by an inner strength that – at the time – I did not understand or know how to explain. God was in control the whole time, preparing my way to show compassion for others in this needy world.

Because of grace, the Lord revealed childhood heroes to me. There was Walt Disney, the creator of a kindly little creature who never hurt a soul. Mickey Mouse would make Einstein's words come to life: "[That] imagination can take you wherever you want to go." Other heroes would influence my life dynamically, just as philanthropist Andrew Carnegie did. Why? Because he donated much of his earnings and lifetime energy to building libraries! Libraries and books would become a sanctuary of sorts until I embraced The Book of Love known as *The Holy Bible*. Arnold Palmer's comebacks, physical strength, yet gentlemanly manner fueled my determination. Frank Sinatra intrigued my imagination by his ability to command a stage, not only with his powerful voice, but his mere presence. He exuded confidence that I wanted to emulate. But it was Perry Como who had more than the smooth baritone pipes; he had class and modesty. Robert F. Kennedy, intelligent and well-spoken showed me passion for what he believed was right and just. His example would guide me several times when faced with a personal or career crisis. He was the quintessential example of a just leader, problem-solver and patriot to his country. Later in life, I desired to speak with his emotion and style.

Books forever remain a steady influence in my life, never my forgetting those adolescent years when Edward Stratemeyer would entertain me with the inquisitive, smart young detectives known as *The Hardy Boys*. As I got more sophisticated, Earl Stanley Gardner would pique my whodunit problem-solving skills with his courtroom drama, featuring the master defense attorney Perry Mason (I tried my best to put such fiction to the test when actually – in real life – being picked to be foreman of a murder trial in common pleas court in my twenties).

Then, of course, there was Ernest Hemingway, who impressed me with *Old Man And The Sea* (later seeing it brought to life on the big screen). Both the book and the movie could hold the attention of its readers and viewers with a solitary scene and character. It made me want to be able to tell a story with that same compelling and convincing nature. Robert Frost, with all his eloquence and prolific writing, would summarize surviving a crisis in simple words: "...and it [life] goes on." Little would I realize how much wisdom is embedded in such a simple truism. When taking some tough hits during my journey, each and every time I would remember life goes on. Frank Sinatra's hit song *That's Life* is practically a personal anthem for me. Jonathan Kellerman would write many detective stories that touched me, for their true life storytelling (just the names changed to protect the innocent – if not the guilty). His compassion for children surviving cancer is a magnificent story in itself. His story writing techniques – so expertly represented by his own academic credentials – is like a course in casework management and clinical psychology combined. It helped me to better understand that everyone has a story when recruiting, hiring, interviewing or coaching someone.

Ralph Waldo Emerson inspired me to have a friend by being a friend. It made me want to be "other-centered." The words and life of Jesus Christ blessed me with wisdom that would remind me of what a friend we have in Jesus. All by the grace of God. It's is more than a song in my heart, it presented an acronym of unselfishness for me to live by: J. O. Y. (Jesus first, then Others, followed by Yourself).

As a young man I had not yet realized that even in the 1960's my life was "moving on and marching forward." I might not have been too sure of where I belonged, but the Good Lord knew who to fit into my life. As my precocious nature developed in high school, my first father figure would come into my life, in the name of Mr. Clarence Duffner: Devoted history teacher and basketball coach. He took this boy, me thinking I was a "reject," and made me special by giving me recognition in front of the entire varsity and junior varsity basketball teams (one who went on to play professional football with the infamous undefeated Miami Dolphins in 1972). He told them that if they had my heart and desire, no one could beat them!

Now, in my life and career coaching, the "heart's desire" has a special place in my ability to understand the central motivational thrusts that people need, to be guided along their vocational pathway. That gentle giant of a man taught me how to shoot baskets, as I have already written about earlier in this book. He made me realize there was something I could do better than anyone else, especially with being so physically and emotionally challenged. This Christian man patiently would tolerate my diatribes, stolen from books – like that of Bertrand Russell, the pipe-toting British philosopher and essayist who wrote *Why I Am Not A Christian*. While questioning God and Christianity, in my own right (wrong as I was), Mr. Duffner showed me how foolish such an educated man like Russell was, being one that never became enlightened by the paradoxes of life.

His contemporary, Alfred North Whitehead, described him well by saying, "It takes an unusual mind to analyze the obvious." Mr. Duffner was a professor of grace! Through his wisdom I would eventually learn that some oddities in life are better accepted – with grace, rather than analyzed. For that reason, I eventually became a Christian. And I did not needlessly keep questioning my origins and circumstances, whether it be why I was placed in a dysfunctional foster home or why I never had survival guilt when cancer did not take my life. In recent years such wisdom has spared me from bitterness when watching my wife suffer privately for so many years. It was grace, more than anything else that guided me to becoming "The Encourager" I am known as today!

Another father figure came into my life after high school graduation, when Mr. James Wilson asked me to come see him at the bank where he was an executive. He wanted to show his appreciation, for having assisted his nephew with his final exams. Mr. Jim Wilson restored my faith in people who make promises and keep them.

As you read earlier, in government, I found that not to be the case. Mr. Wilson and his social worker wife were a generous couple. Their partnership in outreach provided me with fresh perspective from my past, while enabling me to embrace the future with new confidence and self-identity. Their outreach served as a model for the coach I would one day become. I just love helping other people – much of it inspired by that gentleman banker. It was "Mr. Wilson" outside his office. When alone, he invited me to call him Jim.

On my first day as a fellow moneychanger at the historic institution we both worked for, Jim told me, "Never make me look bad. I wouldn't have brought you into the organization if I didn't think you had the right stuff to make for a good banker. I've given you the opportunity. Now it is up to you to develop it."

Banking was my profession of first choice. It educated me well! Mr. Wilson was my first corporate mentor. As my mentor and the uncle to my childhood friends, Tim and Neil (featured in Families of Another Name), there was no way I was going to squander the opportunity.

Friends like Dave, Drew, Don, Bob, Dennis and Neil were and are like brothers to me. They became my family (before I married Connie and actually started my own family), as my foster home became more like my second family. I love my friends. Never will I ever by shy or embarrassed to express those sentiments. I am blessed the way God has brought new friends into my life, especially after Connie's passing: Colin, Adam, Nick, Joshua, Tyler and others. Author and pastor, Charles Swindoll, said it perfectly:

"I cannot even imagine where I would be today were it not for that handful of friends who have given me a heart full of joy. Let's face it, friends make life a lot more fun."

A Victory March

Life is too precious. By the grace of God, my life is surrounded by loving families and incredible friends.

As you have seen, my journey of grace has not been without personal and vocational crises. Adversities and injustices would stalk my pathway. Yet…somehow, feeling like a victim was not an option. For sure, my life has been "out of the ordinary." I do not say extraordinary because it is all relative, isn't it? Everyone has subjective experiences. When they are our own, who are we to say they were worse than that of another? It is, indeed, subjective. Many people – some of notoriety – have told me my story is one of "powerful impact." If so, it sincerely is my prayer that it makes a positive difference in your life. As Alicia Dunham once wrote, "To help someone in need is the surest way to touch God's hand." For sure, it is a sacred privilege for me…for any of us to touch another person's life!

My pathway has had many titles. Personally, I have been enriched by being a husband and a father, to my immediate family and extended (especially to those that I have been a father figure to). Professionally, my life has been enlightened by the realities and lessons learned from the world of work. It has been those realities that summoned me to the mission field, to make a positive difference…to touch lives, to be a banker and a public servant. Ultimately my date with destiny, by the grace of God, was that of being an encourager. I love it! God prepared me well for my final act – my last role. Forever I want to be remembered as The Encourager.

This has been "my pathway to personal enrichment and vocational enlightenment." This has been my story and testimony of God's grace – for His Grace will forever be my anchor. The lessons learned are many!

Some lessons learned came easily. Others were hard, at times quite humbling. It took a lifetime of learning (which goes on) to shape what I call my "guiding principles."

If my story has given you moments of pause and introspection, whereby you feel inspired or motivated to be more enriched and enlightened, then I ask you to be an author of your own life.

Live by your word and God's Word. Share your good news with others. The guiding principles in the next chapter are a summation of what I try to apply every day of my life.

THE ENCOURAGER'S TOP TEN GUIDING PRINCIPLES

1. Prayer is always a first resort, not the last – in good times and tough times.
2. Do not say anything about another person that you would not say to their face.
3. Be other-centered: Make your boss, parent, children, spouse, co-workers, friends, whoever look good.
4. Always look for the good in everybody.
5. Always try to exceed expectations.
6. If you cannot make friends, do not make enemies.
7. Live and learn, but also apply what you learn.
8. Make a smile your logo.
9. Let grace be your guide, giving others a graceful way out of a sticky situation when possible.
10. Make books your friends by taking time to read, so that you can make informed decisions.

My journey has been more than about survival. It's knowing that I was tested in life, sometimes faltering, but always learning from each and every experience and relationship. It's knowing that my core character and true identity would endure tough times, learn from mistakes and be preserved as a living testimony to my friends, family and to those whom I served in the mission of encouragement. It's knowing my Lord and Savior, Jesus Christ. I take comfort now in knowing I do not have to apologize for experience or for being a

Believer. While not pushing religion on anyone, it now means not shirking my duty as a disciple to be a witness of my faith.

It is the knowing that I did not settle for complacency or playing it safe when faced with life-changing decisions or, for that matter, life and death decisions. It means, at times we must make severe sacrifices…paying the price – proving faithfulness, obedience and dependency on God and His plan for our life. It is the knowing that once in childhood and again in my adulthood that I was ready to leave this world and meet my Maker…that I had peace with how I lived my life in the presence of humankind and that of our Almighty.

Perhaps the ultimate lesson learned has been that of understanding our Lord's Prayer, when it teaches us that life is not lived necessarily without evil, but that we will be "delivered" from evil. Oh we of little faith, eh? We all waiver and bend. By the grace of God, we not break.

What about you dear reader? Where are you in your journey? Who are your friends? What do you stand for? Would you be willing to lose everything you worked for…that you own – IF doing the "right thing" meant losing it all? Is your faith strong enough to start all over again if you had to? Can you forgive others that have violated you, personally or otherwise (on the job, in your community, church or at home or school)? Have you lived and learned from life in such a manner that it changed your attitude and behavior?

I agree with what Stephen R. Covey writes in his book, *The Speed of Trust*, "You can't talk your way out of what you've behaved yourself into." Friend, are you ready to leave this world knowing you left behind a legacy of goodwill?

Whatever your station in life, I pray that by reading my book that it felt like you made a new friend. I pray that it encouraged you to have grace revealed in your own life.

YOUR ENCOURAGER,

TESTIMONIALS

"I have never had a conversation with John Klein that has not left me feeling better about myself. I met my friend John at a gym years ago and despite our significant age difference John immediately poured love into me as we talked about my father battling cancer and our strong love for Jesus Christ. It was not the typical conversation one has with a guy at the gym; however, John genuinely cares about people and he is not hesitant to open up and show grace. Throughout the years I have considered John a true encourager and he has helped me as a young man get through the struggles we all face. Life can be tremendously difficult but it helps to know that you have a friend like John in your circle."

-Tyler Suddarth

"I met John in the gym that I worked at, as a personal trainer, nearly 10 years ago. Just like everybody that I met while working in a gym, I intended to motivate and inspire others, including John. However, shortly after meeting him, the roles were mutual, if not reversed. That is, John quickly became a friend and source of inspiration to me in my personal pursuit of inspiring others.

Conversation with John is genuine and he seems an excellent listener to all of those that he speaks with. He is humble and not afraid to share tales of his struggles throughout life, which gives further credence to his journey of becoming a life coach. Beyond the friendship that we had developed over the first few years we knew each other, I looked forward to speaking with John because he always knew how to reassure me with regard to my self-doubt about the professional development that I had embarked upon.

A Victory March

John exudes an enduring sense of compassion, enthusiasm, and pride in helping others help themselves. It is apparent that he places a high value on and gladly accepts his role in helping others achieve what they may sometimes not realize that they are capable of. John truly is and has earned his title of "the encourager.""

-Jason Pawloski, MS, RD

""A Victory March" is a difficult book to put down. The ups and downs of John's life are hard to believe and inspiring at the same time. You always have to read the next page because you want to find out how John overcomes the challenges life presented to him. Reading this book will make you appreciate the positive moments life has to offer. John connects to the reader with his honesty and humor. The stories will lead you to reflect on how you overcome obstacles in your life and inspire you march towards victory and not defeat!"

-Frank Kitchen

"John Klein is the truest definition of the word Leader. Mr. Klein provided me with a lasting fire to be used to light my path of success and sound judgment. Through the use of John's guiding principles I was able to successfully meet my challenges with knowledge and self-worth. John Klein's unique brand of encouragement provided me with a lasting foundation of confidence."

- Anthony Perez, 25 years old, Male

"John Klein, a man who I refer to as "Papa Klein", has the extraordinary ability to connect with the people on a personal level. He has definitely encouraged me to become a better employee, person, and friend. I have never met a person that genuinely gives so freely of himself to help other people on their journey through life. This world would be an amazing place if we had more people like John Klein…A.K.A. the "Encourager.""

-Michael Hartig

"As newlyweds, "A Victory March" by John Klein serves as a great encouragement for our relationship. Through gripping personal testimony, we now understand how God's love and grace can occur - even with the most tragic of life events. We recommend this story to any individual or couple in need of inspiration to step into a deeper relationship with Christ."

– Kirk & Sarah Gagliardo

OTHER PUBLICATIONS BY JOHN J. KLEIN

www.avictorymarch.com/workbook

Your Pathway to Personal Enrichment & Vocational Enlightenment

A better life and career doesn't have to be a lonely journey. This book coaches and encourages you along the way. Everyone has a resume! Some just don't know it yet. Do you know yours? Are you prepared before you send your resume or attend that interview?

JOHN J. KLEIN

Your Pathway to Personal Enrichment and Vocational Enlightenment is a self-help book with two major themes: forces effecting life and career and the need to satisfy one's desire for balance between life at work and home.

Many clients benefited from the proven methods deployed in this book, which combines *analysis* and *intuition*. You will be guided through three freeform exercises, including twenty-seven open-ended questions.

The author has thoroughly explored the world of work, and more importantly - has *lived* the experiences which lend credibility and authenticity to this book. John Klein's personal and vocational life journey is one which has championed just causes. It was, however, not without great sacrifice. His unselfish story of survival, together with lessons learned from the University of Life has prepared him for a new mission field: career coaching and public speaking.

The author's ground zero experience following 9/11 convinced him that our changed world needed more encouragers. A publishing executive saw this book and remarked: *"Just the author's inspiring 'Dedication Page' is worth the cost of the book!"* (Dennison)

"John and his program gave me the chance to see the winner within myself...[his] passion 'to make a difference' gave me the inspiration to want to succeed."
-Mark Surber, Oh.

www.ingramcontent.com/pod-product-compliance
Lightning Source LLC
Chambersburg PA
CBHW070808100426
42742CB00012B/2302